Naomi Slade is a garden expert who works extensively within the gardening and lifestyle media. Previous books include *Dahlias*, *Hydrangeas*, and *Lilies*. For more of her work, visit her website naomislade.com or follow her on Instagram @naomisladegardening and Twitter @naomislade.

Georgianna Lane is a leading floral, garden, and travel photographer whose work has been widely published internationally in books, magazines, and calendars. Her many other books include *Peonies*, *Vintage Roses*, *Hydrangeas*, *Dahlias*, and *Lilies*. Follow Georgianna on Instagram @georgiannalane or visit georgiannalane.com.

LILACS

LILACS

beautiful varieties for home and garden

NAOMI SLADE

photography by

GEORGIANNA LANE

GIBBS SMITH
TO ENRICH AND INSPIRE HUMANKIND

Contents

INTRODUCTION

When the warm spring days arrive and the lilacs burst into bloom, all of nature exhales. For this is a plant that comforts and inspires; it fills the air with nostalgia, marking the passing of time and the changing of the seasons as surely as the chimes of the church bells. Classically elegant, universally loved; cheerful and relaxed; when lilacs are in flower all is as it should be and all is well in the world.

Lilacs in bloom are compelling and ephemeral; captivating in the present but, as a memory, enduring. A flower of then rather than a flower of now. In the mind's eye it is imbued with ghostly beauty; the favorite tree with its enveloping fragrance; a cascade of brilliance and an armful of flowers gaily gathered.

It is an image that infuses daily life – the eponymous color; the popular motif and a familiar flower that is synonymous with an idyll. Yet the season of the flower is short and fleeting, leaving us with an indescribable yearning for lilacs that is akin to *hiraeth*, the Welsh word for which there is no English translation but which represents a spiritual longing for a home that might never have been and a nostalgia for places to which we cannot return.

Even when half-forgotten or left behind, lilacs follow us faithfully. They may fall out of fashion, yet they grow on in parks and old gardens, spilling into the landscape and naturalizing themselves in hedgerows, biding their time and minding their own business.

Native to large swathes of Central and Eastern Europe and to Asia, lilacs are part of the olive family and are closely related to privet,

Ligustrum, with which they share much of their range. In their homelands, it is likely that this pretty – if sometimes scruffy – wild plant has been enjoyed and grown by the local people, without fanfare or record-keeping, for hundreds or even thousands of years. Gradually it ascended to more eminent gardens, and finally to the Courts of Istanbul. Thus, when botanizing Ambassador Ogier Ghiselin, Count de Busbecq, returned to Austria in 1562, among his many treasures was a *lilak*, which he planted in his garden.

Legend has it that when Busbecq relocated to Paris some years later, he took a shoot with him. A humble sprout, perhaps, but the very scion that kick-started the French passion for lilacs. Whether there is a grain of truth in this or not, it was in nineteenth-century France that the lilac underwent its first transformation and luminaries such as the Lemoine family set their sights on creating more numerous and more perfect forms.

Their extensive breeding programs at first focused on the available cultivars of *Syringa vulgaris*, and these were joined by other species as they were discovered and shipped west from Asia. But such was the extent of the Lemoines' success, common old *Syringa vulgaris* is often known as French lilac to this day.

But the lilacs had not stood still. Though adored and feted in France, they moved onwards to neighboring countries and out across the world, to the colonies and new lands of North America, Australia and New Zealand. Soon, they were embraced by other plant breeders. Collections were established; across Europe, in Russia and, particularly, in the USA, where the lilacs that had arrived with the original pioneers had flourished in both the gardens and in the hearts of a country that was styling itself as the land of the free and the home of the brave.

It is hard to pinpoint exactly what has secured the status of *Syringa* as an object of wonder and desire, but its unfussy ways and an appealing habit of erupting into short and glorious bloom, a bold contender for the main event of spring, must certainly have helped. And our pleasure in this has led to a plethora of ornamental and practical uses, such as arranging the flowers prettily on cakes, sprinkling them into the bath or in the creation of a range of medieval concoctions, designed to lower fever, aid digestion, improve the complexion or purge the body of worms.

In more recent history, lilacs became the darlings of popular culture, loved and lauded by songwriters and in poetry. In "The Barrel Organ" by Alfred Noyes, one is exhorted to "Come down to Kew, Kew in lilac time/In lilac time, in lilac time/Come down to Kew in lilac time/(it isn't far from London!)." While, more mournfully, they appear in Walt Whitman's epic and elegiac poem, *When Lilacs Last in the Dooryard Bloom'd*, written on the death of President Lincoln.

In 1919, the flower was adopted as the state flower of New Hampshire, due to its romantic strength of personality, and historian Leon Anderson writes that lilacs are "symbolic of that hardy character of the men and women of the Granite State." They hold similarly mighty sway in Russia, where they are the national flower and symbol of Russian victory in the Second World War.

In the meantime, lilacs have also crept inexorably into folklore, as perverse, contradictory and confusing as any plant can be. On the one hand, white lilac is a symbol of innocence and a celebration of new life and new love. On the other, a girl who wears a sprig of lilac will never get married, and anyone who received a bunch of lilacs from their betrothed could consider the impending nuptials canceled. Like other white flowers, such as snowdrops and lilies, there is a superstition that bringing lilacs into the house spells ill fortune, while an association with funerals has arisen from the old custom of lining coffins with white lilac, the perfume masking, to a certain extent, the odors of putrefaction.

In Persian, the word *lilak* or *lilaf*, means "bluish," and this, in various forms, is how lilacs are known across Europe. The botanical name, *Syringa*, however, comes from another story.

In Greek legend, Syrinx was a nymph and chaste follower of Artemis. Pursued by Pan, the amorous god of nature and wild places, she rushed to the river's edge where the river nymphs took pity on her and turned her into a reed. Frustrated at his loss, the deity picked the reed and turned it into a pipe that played a whispering, echoing tune. In some versions she lives on in the music or is with him forever in the pipes, as he wanders the hills; captured in the music but with her chastity intact.

Related to this, in England an early common name for lilac was pipe tree or blow stem, because although they are woody, lilac twigs

are filled with a soft pith, which can be easily removed to create a hollow reed.

A mishmash of common and Latin names is not unusual when it comes to plants. The tides of botany and horticultural habit are inconstant and there is ongoing debate, across the board, as to what should be classified as part of which genus. The name *Syringa* was at one time also used for mock orange, now *Philadelphus*, which has similar pithy stems, meanwhile, migrating gardeners see a plant and speak as they find. This gives us a range of visually vaguely similar but unrelated pretenders to the lilac name, including *Ceanothus*, which is known as Californian lilac; *Hebe hulkeana*, the New Zealand Lilac, and *Hardenbergia violacea* or Australian lilac.

Fashion is fickle and, as the twentieth century wore on, the first lilac-breeding pioneers gradually faded away and a number of collections diminished or vanished. Perhaps they were a victim of their very familiarity, too well-known and insufficiently exotic to preserve. In England they ebbed gracefully; the legendary lilacs of Kew are now few and far between. And although lilac festivals carry the torch in the USA, the notable garden of breeder Hulda Klager, already lost once to flood, was only just rescued from the brink of a second destruction.

Then, like a fragrant, floral phoenix, lilacs rose again. Venerated once more as the most romantic flower of late spring and early summer, cooed over on social media, cut in armfuls for a vase full of sweetness and enjoyed for their lavishness.

It is a foppish sort of plant; it flowers only briefly and can grow like a weed if you let it, but the lilac has us firmly in its thrall. It is loved for its vintage looks and perfume; received with applause and glad cries wherever it goes. Comforting, reliable, romantic and almost always socially appropriate, the vast froufrou flowers are adored by brides and florists. And in close-up one can be lost in the detail of tiny tubular flowers, so subtle and modest, so varied, and borne on a plant that is both hardy and carefree.

A plant that gives us spectacular blooms that rise to the clarion call of spring and then fade charmingly into the background. Not a diva but an accomplished performer that knows her part backwards and delivers a polished turn, magnificently, every time. Evocative, poignant, fleeting and hardy, lilacs are loved because they remind us of something very visceral. They take their place and mark the cycle of life, and it has always been so.

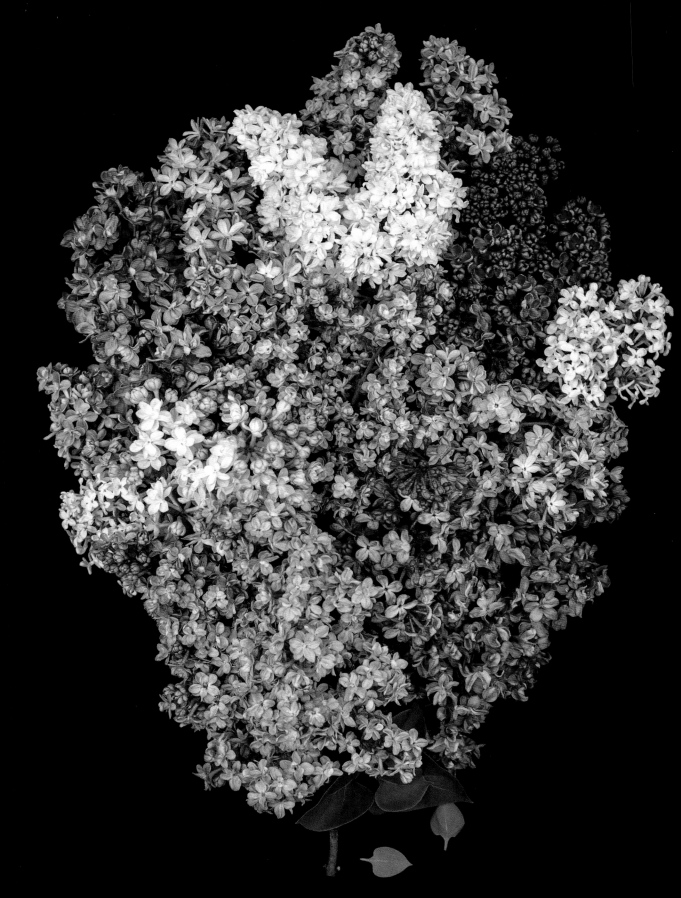

THE HISTORY AND BOTANY OF LILACS

THE LILAC IS THE FLOWER OF ITS MOMENT. GLORIOUS, SOPHISTICATED AND EPHEMERAL, IT TRANSCENDS ITS SURROUNDINGS AND CAPTIVATES ITS ADMIRERS WHO, THOUGH THEY MAY DRIFT AWAY, WILL ALWAYS RETURN. MODERN, VINTAGE AND EVERYTHING IN BETWEEN, IT RISES TO EVERY OCCASION AND TEASES US WITH ITS SECRETS AND LEGENDS: A FRAGRANT PIONEER THAT HAS CONQUERED THE WORLD, YET STILL FINDS A WELCOME IN HOMES AND GARDENS WHEREVER IT GOES.

Glorious, romantic, richly scented and timeless, lilacs are loved by all. Erupting out of hedgerows or sprawling casually around gardens, they are an instantly recognizable highlight of the late spring season. But, despite significant advances in breeding, and the availability of eminently garden-worthy plants, lilacs have found themselves overlooked, betimes; the fanfare of horticulture saved for roses, clematis, peonies and other flamboyant sources of temptation.

An easy-going and prolific plant, lilac hails from Eastern Europe and Asia and it is now found all over the world, wherever climate permits. Few would fail to identify a plant that is culturally embedded to this extent, but it is those places like France, the Americas and Russia, where there is a tradition of *Syringa* breeding, that the flame of public passion burns brightest.

The majority of the 25 lilac species currently recognized are native to mountainous areas of Central Asia, running from Afghanistan in the west, through China and the Himalayas to Korea and the islands of Japan. A further two species are found in Eastern Europe – *Syringa vulgaris*, the so-called "common lilac," which is native to Balkan countries such as Serbia, Macedonia and Romania and throughout Southeastern Europe, and *S. josikaea*, or the Hungarian lilac, which is found more locally in Romania, the Czech Republic and Slovakia and other parts of the former Austro-Hungarian Empire.

From wilderness to cultivation

When a species is spread over a wide area, the natural variation can be substantial. Differences in local environment can cause even closely related individuals to grow in different ways, and with well-dispersed populations that are subject to a range of selection pressures and local clusters of mutation, it can be hard for the isolated plant hunter halfway up a mountain to be certain what it is they have found.

The scope for natural variation was observed in a captive collection in the 1930s, by Dr Edgar Anderson, arborist at the Arnold Arboretum of Harvard University, Boston, USA. Having studied a number of wild European lilacs, forms of *Syringa vulgaris*, he wrote, "Their flowers are not borne in bunches but in great open sprays. The panicles may reach two feet in length. Nor does the general form of the bush follow closely a single pattern, as in the cultivated lilac."

As a result, large numbers of species and subspecies have been historically identified. These are made up of related plants collected in different areas and joining the accession lists in different gardens. Ironing out the wrinkles of what is sufficiently different, and what is not, is an ongoing and rather enjoyable job for students of genetics and botany the world over.

According to the International Lilac Society, at the time of writing there are four series of lilacs below the level of the genus *Syringa* – *Syringa*, *Ligustrina*, *Pubescentes* and *Villosae* – which don't interbreed. On the taxonomic level below this, there are 15 natural species, three natural hybrid species, seven man-made hybrid species and a number of subspecies – though not all these are commercially available.

Lilacs cultivated for the garden have been selected for uniformity, distinctiveness and flower size, *inter alia*, and now look very different from their wild brethren. And although *Syringa vulgaris* is found naturalized both in Western Europe and in North America, these plants are the escapee seedlings of the cultivated lilacs of yore.

The precise moment when a particularly fine specimen of *Syringa vulgaris* stepped from its wild home, perhaps beside a rocky path in the Balkans, to the nurturing confines of a garden is shrouded in the mists of time. But as early as the mid-sixteenth century, scholars were describing plants that sound very like lilacs, growing in the gardens of Istanbul.

It is no great feat to imagine an attractive local flower being quietly cultivated for decades without coming to the attention of Western scribes. Visiting friends and relatives might have departed with a shoot or two to grow on elsewhere, so gaining currency as a cherished ornamental, the choicest *Syringa* could have covered quite some distance. Indeed, lilacs are not generally found wild in modern Turkey, although it grows there as a garden plant.

In the 1550s, Ambassador Ogier Ghiselin, Count de Busbecq, was sent by Ferdinand I of Austria to represent him at the Court of Süleyman the Magnificent. A diplomat and naturalist, Busbecq was an intellectually curious man and an avid collector of many things, including plants. He is credited with bringing *Lilium chalcedonicum* and tulips back to Vienna and it is thought that *lilak* or *Türkischer holler* or *holunder* (Turkish elderberry) as he called it, was among his hoard.

In 1570, Busbecq made a permanent move from Vienna to France, accompanying Archduchess Elizabeth, who was to marry King Charles IX. Legend has it that the lilac was included among the plants in his luggage, which is how it arrived in Paris.

Whether it was the work of a single plant-obsessed ambassador, or whether by more circuitous means, lilacs were embraced in France from the sixteenth century onwards. They were bred and improved upon in gardens far and wide. The clusters of flowers became larger, as did the individual florets; double forms appeared and the color palette was extended from lilac and white, to pink, mauve, magenta and violet.

Having shuffled slightly uncertainly into the botanical literature of its day, it was as a garden

plant that the lilac became established, making its merry way to Holland, Sweden and Finland, to England, and onwards to various colonies and outposts with settlers and migrants. Indeed, it was over a century before wild *Syringa vulgaris* was eventually tracked down, discovered in its mountain fastness, by British botanist John Sibthorp, in 1794, when traveling from northern Bulgaria to Istanbul. This was corroborated by Anton Rochel in 1828, who found it in western Romania, and János Heuffel, who identified the plant in various locations in Hungary.

As a cultivated plant, it was by now appearing regularly in herbals and other missives. In his seventeenth-century herbal, notable English botanist John Parkinson described a pipe tree that carried "blew or violet colored flowers on a long stalke, of the bignesse and fashion of a Foxe taile." And international distribution must have been rapid. Just a century or so later, in 1753, as part of the exciting trade in horticultural rarities between the continents, London-based Quaker and wool merchant Peter Collinson sent lilacs to American botanist John Bartram, only to have Bartram churlishly complain that "lilacs are already too numerous, as roots brought by the early settlers have spread enormously."

While plant hunting is often considered a Victorian pastime, the earlier period of commercial and political exploration known as the Age of Reason also introduced novelties to Western Europe.

A notable contributor was Pierre d'Incarville, a French Jesuit missionary and botanist, who discovered *Syringa pekinensis* in the mountains near Beijing in 1742, then went on to find *S. villosa* in the same area in 1750.

It was then nearly 100 years before the *Syringa emodi* was discovered in Afghanistan, in around 1831, but by now plant-hunting fever was gathering momentum. *Syringa oblata* was sent back to England from China by Robert Fortune in the early 1850s; *Syringa pubescens* arrived in the early 1880s and this was followed, in turn, by *S. yunnanensis* and *S. villosa*.

It was an internationally tumultuous time. Borders opened and were defended; wars were fought. Treaties were drawn up, alliances forged, and a veritable horde of collectors rampaged into Asia. As a result, certain species were collected several times in several different places on behalf of a range of sponsors. The names of many botanizing legends of the period have achieved immortality in now-familiar garden plants: Pierre d'Incarville, Père Jean Marie Delavay and Père David from France; Robert Fortune, George Forrest and Ernest Wilson from the UK; while Russian collectors included Grigorii Potanin, Karl Maximowicz and Vladimir Komarov.

Thanks in large part to the accepted narrative and the literature of the time, it is tempting to consider horticulture and plant hunting from the perspective of Western Europe, but that does the rest of the world a huge disservice. Firstly, the perpetrators of plant hunting were immensely well-traveled and very often spent years or decades living and working in countries other than that of their birth. Those that survived often became supremely well-connected, but essentially rootless.

Other countries, meanwhile, had their eyes on potential opportunities and, as the British Crown took control of India, the incumbent generals were alarmed to discover that Czar Alexander II was deploying military botanists to newly open China, from where they sent many thousands of plants back to Russia.

The USA, too, was far from sleeping, and while Ernest "Chinese" Wilson collected hundreds of plants, including lilacs, while working for the Veitch Nursery near London, he later changed his allegiance to the Arnold Arboretum, Massachusetts. Meanwhile *Syringa meyeri,* now known as *S. pubescens* subsp. *pubescens*, was discovered as a garden plant, "found" by Frank Meyer (Dutch by birth and American by inclination) in a garden near Beijing.

And although the cultivation and use of lilacs in their native Asian countries has historically been something of a closed book to Western observers, it is known that *Syringa meyeri* has been grown as a garden specimen, and *S. pekinensis* too, and it seems unlikely that the horticulturists of the region, with their passion for blossom and talent for perfection, can have been entirely indifferent to the charm of lilacs.

Lilac breeders: in pursuit of perfection

While lilacs are widely known and widely loved, in some places they are held in greater esteem than in others. This is in part due to culture and habit and in part due to marketing: when breeders and nurserymen trumpet their plants to the masses, enthusiasm and uptake increase and the credibility and desirability of these specimens rises.

As it also embraced hydrangeas, France embraced lilacs, becoming a hotbed of lilac passion to the point where *Syringa vulgaris* is still generically known as French lilac. The USA and Canada, together with Russia, also fell in love and developed their own breeding tradition, producing notable cultivars and new varieties apace.

Plant breeders seek to combine desirable qualities of individuals to create better, more garden-worthy forms. Looks are important, certainly, and much breeding is undertaken to create bigger flowers, double forms and unusual colors. But there are other characteristics that can be selected for as well, such as the size of the plant, its health and disease resistance, and its ability to extend the season of interest with plants that bloom earlier or later than the norm.

There are various ways to go about creating a "better" plant. Firstly, you can simply take the finest of the mixed bag of seedlings or wild plants you have available and propagate vegetatively from these. Alternatively, you can look out for natural mutations or sports; these usually arise as a "different-looking" section on the parent plant, which, if attractive, can be cloned to conserve the new characteristic.

Taking a more scientific approach, however, reduces the element of chance. If you know what combination of characteristics you hope to end up with, for example small size and huge flowers, you pick parents that each express these strongly. You might, therefore, choose a very dwarf variety with average-sized flowers, to partner with a leggy, but large-flowered specimen. Pollen is then transferred from the anther of the pollen parent to the stigma of a flower on the seed parent.

The resulting seeds are hybrids that combine parental qualities in various ways. These can be grown on until they reveal their character, and the most promising can then be back-crossed with a parent to further enhance the desired qualities, or crossed with another plant to introduce a new variable – double flowers, perhaps.

Much of the early breeding work on *Syringa* was carried out, as discussed, in France; most notably by the Lemoine family. In the nineteenth century, Victor Lemoine and his wife Marie carried out the first extensive breeding program at their nursery in Nancy. This created the first large-flowered double lilacs and the *hyacinthiflora* hybrids.

A keen plantsman, Victor had acquired an unusual, blue, double lilac, *Syringa vulgaris* 'Azurea Plena' and, although the job was awkward and fiddly, he pollinated the flowers – or rather, because Marie was younger and had small hands, he got her to climb a ladder and do it – with the very best single forms of *S. vulgaris* then available. Later, when early flowering *Syringa oblata* arrived from China, he brought that into the mix, too.

Having created some beautiful double plants, Victor and Marie crossed them again, with the finest single lilacs they could lay their hands on. When Victor died in 1911, the work was continued by his son Émile and grandson Henri. And although the nursery closed in 1955, their legacy is remarkable, introducing at least 214 Lemoine lilacs over a period of nearly 80 years. Many of these are still available, including deep blue 'Président Grévy' (page 101), magenta 'Charles Joly' (page 64) and white 'Madame Lemoine' (page 203).

A number of other nurseries in Europe also worked with lilacs in the late nineteenth and early twentieth centuries. Luminaries included German breeders Franz and Helmutt Ludwig Späth, and Florent Stepman-Demessemaeker in Belgium, and there was a flurry of activity in Dutch nursery families around the Aalsmeer and Boskoop regions – famously epicenters of floristry and nursery production.

Lilacs had long been popular in North America, however, and in the early twentieth century there was a noticeable upswelling of hybridization work there, as well.

In the 1890s Scotsman John Dunbar created the now-famous lilac garden at Highland Park in Rochester, New York. His early planting of around a hundred shrubs soon flowered magnificently, attracting flocks of admirers and initiating the Rochester Lilac Festival that continues to this day (page 30). Over time, he raised a number of open-pollinated seedlings, selecting 19 to be named, including deep purple 'Adelaide Dunbar' (page 108) and pink 'General Sherman', while 'President Lincoln' (page 82), introduced in 1916, went on to become one of the most popular lilacs of all time and a valuable breeding parent in its own right.

Queen among plant breeders, Isabella Preston must have been a force to be reckoned with, born in 1881 and making a name for herself at a point where it was difficult for a woman to get any sort of equality, let alone paid employment in scientific circles. Studying horticulture first in England then in Canada at Ontario Agricultural College, she spent her career creating outstanding garden plants including roses, crab apples, lilies and, in the 1920s, a line of lilacs called the Preston Lilacs – *Syringa × prestoniae*. Often named after Shakespearean heroines such as Desdemona and Juliet, these plants are characteristically tall, late-blooming and very winter hardy.

And there is another doyenne of lilacs in the American hall of fame. Hulda Klager was born in Germany and moved to the USA as a baby. When she married, she promptly planted a garden, and her dairyman husband, who clearly knew the value of a happy wife, defended both house and plot from annual flooding by the Lewis River with an embankment 7 feet high.

Although she had little formal education, Hulda was a self-taught botanist and read every gardening manual she could lay her hands on. This included a book called *New Creations in Plant Life*, published in 1905, which explained about cross-pollinating plants.

The same year, she purchased seven named varieties of *Syringa vulgaris* and started experimenting. She threw two away, unimpressed by the quality of flowers, and marauding horses destroyed a couple more; but from the remaining "magic three" she created over 100 new cultivars and established a lilac garden and nursery business at Woodland, her parents' original home. Unfortunately, the garden was destroyed by a catastrophic flood in 1948, but although she was aged 84 by then, she set out to rebuild it and it has since become a State and National Historic Site.

It was the search for good, ornamental plants that would withstand the rigors of a Canadian winter that inspired Manitoba cattle rancher Frank Leith Skinner, who, similarly, taught himself the theory and got cracking. With a nursery that was once famous worldwide as a source of hardy fruit trees and garden plants, he also introduced a line of 'American Lilacs', including the popular classic 'Maiden's Blush' (page 156) and winter-hardy and early flowering *Syringa ×hyacinthiflora* hybrids. The Frank Skinner Arboretum Trail still exists today.

The American interest in lilac breeding continued throughout the twentieth century, on a professional, amateur and have-a-go-hero basis, but a particular pioneer was parish priest, professor and author of *Lilacs: A Gardener's Encyclopedia*, John Fiala, who was also a founding director of the International Lilac Society.

In the 1950s he became interested in the potential for genetic manipulation using colchicine, which is a toxic substance derived from the autumn-flowering bulb *Colchicum*, which disrupts cell division and causes mutations. While his results were modest, he appears to have demonstrated that significant changes can be achieved in this way, particularly with the introduction of golden-leaved variety 'Kum-Bum'. In total he was responsible for the introduction of nearly 100 lilac cultivars and his legacy includes dwarf variety 'Pixie' and a range of blues, such as 'Wedgewood Blue'.

While information has only become available in the last 40 or 50 years, it seems there was a parallel tradition of trendsetting lilac breeders in Russia and its neighboring countries. Though politics, language difficulties and import barriers have historically held up an exchange in knowledge and plants between enthusiasts on opposite sides of the Iron Curtain, there have been several notable hybridizers, including the early pioneer Nikolai Kuzmich Vekhov (1887–1956) and his eminent successor Leonid Kolesnikov.

A horticultural trailblazer and innovator, Leonid was, from his youth, an avid collector and student of all things *Syringa* and, although his work was interrupted by the Second World War, in which he was severely wounded, he introduced 'Krasavitsa Moskvy' or 'Beauty of Moscow' (page 40) in 1947. He is also responsible for purple 'Znamya Lenina' or 'Banner of Lenin' (page 196) and the double blue lilac, 'Nadezhda' (page 48), which translates as 'Hope'.

To this day, lilac research and display are supported by the Russian government and universities. In particular, the 'Russian Lilac' breeding group from Moscow, made up of Sergei Aladin, Olga Aladina, Tatyana Polyakova and Anastasia Aladina, has released in the region of 200 new lilacs since 2009. Although only a limited number of these cultivars is available to gardeners elsewhere in the world, their continued work and prodigious output has led to flattering comparisons with the Lemoine family.

GOOD ENOUGH TO EAT

Lilac flowers are edible and, like calendula, nasturtiums, rose petals and violets, can be used to decorate cakes or used as a garnish in salads. If you are feeling creative, experiment with making lilac-infused vinegar or lilac sugar, for cooking or sprinkling.

The blooms can also be used for drinks, infused as a refreshing perfumed tea or, like elderflowers, combined with sugar, water and lemon for a syrup or cordial.

Perfumes vary and some varieties are more flavorful than others, so sample them first to check that you like them. It is also worth experimenting to find out how powerful – or overpowering – they may be, and therefore how much you want to use!

Choose attractive, healthy flowers that have not been sprayed with any chemicals. Pick the flowers soon after opening and give them a rinse if they are dusty, then use the individual florets or thyrses (page 25) according to your taste.

Anatomy of a lilac

The genus *Syringa* falls within the *Oleaceae* – the olive family – which includes other well-known garden plants such as forsythia, jasmine and ash (*Fraxinus*), together with privet or *Ligustrum*, which is particularly closely related and has been used as a rootstock for grafted lilacs. While this may seem a diverse group of plants, the family resemblance can be seen in the flowers, all of which are four-petaled.

Lilacs are woody plants and are generally grown as shrubs and small trees. The division between the two is often visually indistinct, but tree lilacs can reach around 25 feet, while shrubs may be around 12 feet. Dwarf varieties are smaller and more compact still.

The basic arrangement of the plant is usually a number of woody stems, emerging from the ground and then branching to create a dense, twiggy canopy. The leaves are arranged in pairs along the stem. Those of the common lilac, *Syringa vulgaris*, are of average size, with smooth edges that taper to a point. There is, however, a certain amount of variation between the species, so *Syringa meyeri* (syn. *S. pubescens* subsp. *pubescens*) has small, rounded leaves and other less well-known varieties such as *S. × laciniata* and *S. pinnatifolia* can have leaves that are feathered or lobed. There are also selections where the usually mid-green leaves are variegated or golden in color.

The flowers are produced on the previous season's growth and are borne in large, conical clusters or panicles, properly known as thyrses. Insect-pollinated and usually fragrant, the individual florets are tubular in shape and typically have four petals, although double flowers have more. The shape of the petals can be highly variable and they may be rounded, pointed, cupped, reflexed or even divided. When the flowers fade, they leave behind small, brown seed capsules.

As a lilac establishes, it develops a number of deep anchoring roots to stabilize the plant, and a network of shallow, fibrous, feeding roots, through which it takes up water and nutrients from the soil.

COLOR CARE

One of the most significant aspects of a lilac flower is its color. Aficionados use an official classification system called the Wister Code, that ranks color on a scale of I–VII: White, Violet, Bluish, Lilac, Pinkish, Magenta and Purple.

According to observers, the color of lilacs can vary slightly, from year to year and location to location; it is also said that soil pH may have a minor effect, and that extremes will create a muddy hue. Specimens planted in neutral or slightly alkaline soils are thought to have the best and clearest color.

Very bright light will often cause the color in the delicate petals to fade, so aim for a little midday shade in a south-facing spot.

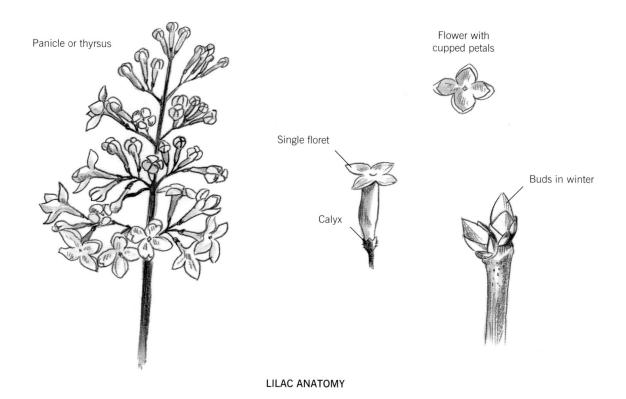

Panicle or thyrsus

Flower with cupped petals

Single floret

Calyx

Buds in winter

LILAC ANATOMY

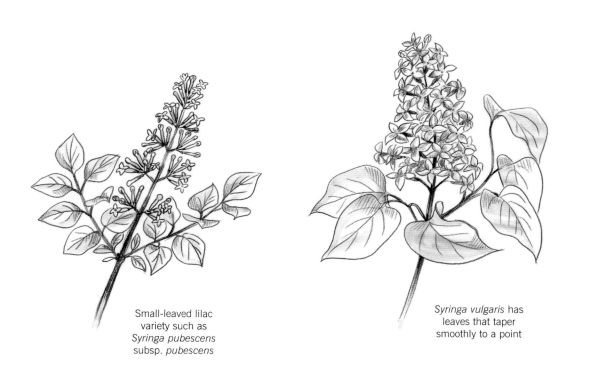

Small-leaved lilac variety such as *Syringa pubescens* subsp. *pubescens*

Syringa vulgaris has leaves that taper smoothly to a point

Designing with lilacs

When adding lilacs to a planting scheme or working to improve the aesthetic qualities of those that are already there, it's worth giving some thought to how they behave. Planting shrubs and trees should be viewed as a long-term commitment, and although they can be moved if necessary, putting them in the right place first time around can save time and energy, and will make for a healthier, happier plant.

Many lilacs grow to be fairly large, so they need to be considered in the context of the landscape, and even if the chosen variety is small, when used in a small garden it will still have a presence within that space. This is a shrub whose core appeal lies in the glorious, magnificent floral display in late spring or early summer, yet this is relatively brief, and when it is gone, you need to consider what is there for the rest of the year – in most cases this will be a dense green bush that will need to integrate with other garden highlights.

So, when siting your lilac, in addition to attending to its fundamental needs of plenty of sun and good drainage, give it sufficient space to grow. You can always edge perennials away from the plant as it matures, but this is harder to do with other, complementary, shrubs, which may be both sizable and vital to the design.

It therefore pays to give consideration to not just the lilac itself, but also to its supporting cast and how it deports itself as part of the wider garden.

Consider also how you plan to use the space and how the lilac will be enjoyed. Sited next to the terrace or near a window, the glorious scent can be appreciated. And while white flowers will shine beautifully against a dark backdrop of evergreens or a painted fence, the more subtle dark purples will be lost.

After flowering, some lilac cultivars such as *Syringa* ×*hyacinthiflora, S. meyeri* (syn. *S. pubescens* subsp. *pubescens*) and *S. pubescens* subsp. *patula* will have a modest renaissance in autumn as the leaves change color, but for experienced gardeners, choosing a lilac with unusually shaped or colored leaves can extend the interest, too. *Syringa* 'Kum-Bum' has golden foliage while *S. vulgaris* 'Aucubaefolia' and *S. emodi* 'Variegata' are variegated gold and green; like other yellow-leaved plants, these should be sited in full sun. Divided and cut-leaved varieties include *Syringa* × *laciniata, S. pinnatifolia* and ferny *S. protolaciniata*.

A simple, classic and popular way to use a lilac is as a specimen. They are often planted in a lawn, singly or as part of a collection, which can be selected to flower in series. The season of interest can be further extended with spring and autumn bulbs, naturalized in the grass.

Lilac varieties not prone to suckering can work as an accent plant in an herbaceous scheme, where they will put on a show and then fade into the background, to allow the summer and autumn flowers to do their thing. In either case, the plant can be left in its natural, bushy state, or the lower branches pruned to create an upright, leggy, multi-stemmed plant, more reminiscent of a small tree.

In an herbaceous border it is important to choose robust companion plants that will do well in the often drier, shadier environment near the shrub. Consider *Geranium phaeum*, forget-me-not and campanula. If you have lifted the crown by cutting back the lower branches to let in the sun, surround your lilac with alliums and tulips in harmonious colors of pink, white and plum, and follow these with lilies or hardy geraniums. You could also team a large lilac with lower-growing foliage interest, planting boldly variegated hostas and compact *Hydrangea serrata* cultivars.

An interesting and unexpected use for lilacs is as an informal hedge. Dense, hardy, disease-resistant varieties such as *Syringa josikaea* and *S.* × *chinensis* are ideal along the edge of a path, used as a boundary within a landscape, in a front garden or to shield a parking area. For a uniform look, plant them at one or two plants per 3¼ feet. Don't prune out the suckers that arise from the base, as these will help create a dense thicket, but do remember to tidy and reshape the hedge after flowering.

To mix things up a bit, lilacs will excel when combined with plants of a similar habit, in a shrub border or as a loose screen. Grow them alongside woody companions such as *Amelanchier*, *Viburnum* × *bodnantense* 'Dawn', crab apples or the larger hydrangeas, or shrubs and small trees with interesting and colored foliage, for example *Sambucus nigra* 'Black Lace'. Rosehips and berries are also useful for a varied effect with a longer period of interest.

But there are some garden companions with which a lilac should not lightly associate. The airy, sophisticated flowers of *Syringa* create a haze of color, not an explosion, and this can be easily eclipsed by some of their more brash seasonal contemporaries. Even in a mixed planting scheme, be careful about pitching them in floral battle against bright orange azaleas or neon pink camelias: they are unlikely to come out of it well and it would be a sad waste of their charms.

While many lilacs are too large to be considered as container specimens, a number of dwarf varieties, such as *Syringa* 'Red Pixie', *S. vulgaris* 'Munchkin' or *S. meyeri* 'Palibin', will lend themselves to being planted in a large pot or in a raised bed. While these plants do have the potential to grow, they can be kept reasonably compact with annual pruning. Even so, it pays to choose the biggest container you can manage, at least 12 inches deep and 2 feet wide, to accommodate those spreading roots, and preferably larger still – unless you want to develop your skills and grow the plant as a bonsai.

FLOWER ARRANGING

Lilacs make wonderful cut flowers. The strong, woody stems resist wilting and carry the weighty blooms with ease, meaning that when gathered by the armful and piled into big jugs and buckets, they make a magnificent arrangement with no effort at all.

Cut lilacs early in the day, while the air is still cool and the cells of the plant are still plump and full of water. Select flowers that are nice and fresh and that have a number of buds that are yet to open; this will help prolong the display. Cutting flowers is a form of pruning, or early deadheading, so use the opportunity to shape the plant where possible, even if you need to come back to finish the job later.

Take a clean pail of cool water into the garden with you and, as you cut the stems, plunge them straight into it. When you are done, leave the bucket of flowers in a cool, dark place for several hours or overnight, so they have a chance to have a long drink and recover.

When you are ready to arrange the lilacs, cut the stems again, while they are still underwater, at an angle of about 45 degrees. It is sometimes suggested that woody-stemmed flowers such as lilacs and roses should have the bottom of the stem hammered to aid the take-up of water, but this is not necessary.

Strip off any lower foliage that is not necessary for the look of the arrangement. Submerged leaves will start to rot and foliage will also compete with the flowers for water. If the lilacs start to look tired after a day or so, they often perk up if the stems are re-cut and the water refreshed.

Arrange the lilacs to your satisfaction in a vase that has been scrupulously cleaned, then filled with clean water. A drop of bleach or teaspoon of vinegar will inhibit bacterial growth and help the flowers to last longer. A simple cluster of lilacs, of any color, will look wonderful, but they are also fantastic as part of a combination. Team them with inky purple tulips and branches of apple blossom or the bronzy young foliage of *Physocarpus opulifolius* 'Diabolo'; experiment by adding other seasonal flowers, such as ranunculus, *Geranium phaeum* and aquilegia; or rounded alliums and tall foxgloves. Ferns and evergreen foliage make an excellent foil.

Societies and organizations

Such is the popularity of lilacs that a number of societies, gardens, festivals and collections have arisen around the world. These are a great resource to the lilac grower and if you want to know more about this beguiling plant, visit gardens and celebrations, and meet other enthusiasts and experts, then these should be your first stop.

THE INTERNATIONAL LILAC SOCIETY

Incorporated in 1971, the ILS is comprised of people who share a particular appreciation and fondness of the lilac and wish to broaden understanding and awareness of the genus. An annual convention is held in lilac season and a range of resources is available on the website. www.internationallilacsociety.org

GARDENS AND COLLECTIONS

There are a large number of lilac gardens, ranging from personal projects to substantial scientific resources. The list below gives a flavor of what is available, but it is far from comprehensive. Making contacts in lilac circles and doing some internet research will reveal further gems, both in the countries listed here and elsewhere in the world.

United States of America

Arnold Arboretum, Boston, Massachusetts: One of the oldest and largest collections of lilacs in America. Their Lilac Sunday event is celebrated on the second Sunday in May. www.arboretum.harvard.edu

The Hulda Klager Garden, Woodland, Washington: A restoration project to honor the work of famed lilac breeder, Hulda Klager. Each year they host a number of Lilac Days to celebrate the flower in bloom. www.lilacgardens.com

Rochester Lilac Festival, Highland Park, Rochester, New York: The biggest free festival of its kind, held annually in May. https://rochesterevents.com/lilac-festival/

Wolcott Lilac Garden, Kent, Ohio: An historic garden and personal lilac collection of Robert Zavodny, President of the International Lilac Society. www.wolcottlilacgardens.org

Canada

Le Musée des Lilas, Saint-Georges de Beauce, Quebec. A living museum of lilacs with one of the largest collections of cultivars in the world. www.thelilacmuseum.com

Royal Botanical Gardens, Hamilton, Ontario. One of the largest and most diverse lilac collections in the world. They host a Lilac Celebration in May. www.rbg.ca

Central Experimental Farm, Ottawa, Ontario. An extensive collection of lilacs, located in a number of areas around the site. www.friendsofthefarm.ca

United Kingdom

The Lilac Walk at Golden Acre Park, Leeds, Yorkshire: A Plant Heritage National Collection of lilacs that is managed by Leeds City Council. www.plantheritage.org.uk

France

Conservatoire et Jardins Botaniques de Nancy: A large collection featuring many varieties bred by the Lemoine family who operated locally. www.jardinbotaniquedenancy.eu

Jardins de Brocéliande, Bréal-sous-Montfort, Brittany: An impressive collection numbering around 450 varieties. www.jardinsdebroceliande.fr/jardin/les-lilas

Russia

Peter the Great Botanic Garden, St Petersburg: Founded by Peter I in 1714 as an apothecary garden and collection of rare and interesting foreign plants, it later became a research facility. www.saint-petersburg.com/parks/botanical-garden

Moscow State University The Apothecaries' Garden, Moscow: One of the oldest botanical institutions in Russia, dating from 1706, it contains around 200 lilac cultivars. www.herba.msu.ru/departments/garden; www.hortus.ru/en

Russian Academy of Sciences in Moscow: An impressive and extensive scientific collection of plants, containing about 200 lilac cultivars. www.gbsad.ru

Japan

Sapporo Parks, Japan: With about 300 cultivars in total, an annual Lilac Festival is held across two parks – Odori Park, which is home to more than 400 lilac trees, and Kawashimo Park, which contains around 1,700 lilac trees. https://hokkaidoguide.com/lilac-spring-festival/

Fantastic Frills

Katherine Havemeyer

A fine and glamorous plant, Katherine Havemeyer is a Lemoine cultivar, which arrived on the gardening scene in 1922.

The thyrses are huge and heavy, and uneven magenta buds open into untidy, somewhat double flowers in a medley of subtle shades, reminiscent of summer-fruit sorbet.

Enduringly popular, *Syringa vulgaris* 'Katherine Havemeyer' received the RHS Award of Garden Merit in 1933 and again in 1969. It is, however, susceptible to leaf roll necrosis, so avoid sites that suffer from air pollution.

....

Syringa vulgaris 'Katherine Havemeyer'
Height Up to 13 ft
Spread Up to 13 ft
Flower size Very large
Scent Immensely fragrant
Color Lavender-pink or purple
Foliage Heart-shaped, soft-green leaves
In the garden A bit of a stunner
As a cut flower Absolutely beautiful

Krasavitsa Moskvy
syn. Beauty of Moscow

Russian breeder Leonid Kolesnikov is something of a legend in lilac circles, and although he is credited with the introduction of many excellent plants, Beauty of Moscow really lives up to its name.

The smoky-pink buds are loosely packed and, as they start to swell, they lighten to pale lavender and shell pink, then unfurl to reveal double flowers of the purest white. The result is a frothy panicle that is beautifully two-toned and textured, the shadows of pink emphasizing the pearly white in a flower that is elegant, airy and ultimately desirable.

So lovely is this flower, in fact, that it is available all over the world; known as Krasavitsa Moskvy in Russia, Belle de Moscou in France, and in Germany variously as Schöne von Moskau and Mädchen aus Moskau.

Use this lilac as a landscape shrub, or tuck it into a corner of a smaller garden and plant around it with complementary perennials and climbers to extend the season.

Introduced in 1947, Beauty of Moscow has received an RHS Award of Garden Merit.

....

Syringa vulgaris 'Krasavitsa Moskvy' syn. 'Beauty of Moscow'
Height 10–13 ft
Spread 6½–10 ft
Flower size Large
Scent A sweet fragrance that intensifies with maturity
Color Pale pink fading to white
Foliage Apple green
In the garden Very much worth the space
As a cut flower Gather it in armfuls and enjoy

Paul Thirion

Gorgeously lavish and outstandingly lush, lilac Paul Thirion is magnificent as a cut flower and works fabulously well in the garden, too.

The buds are a delicious, deep carmine-pink, borne in heavy trusses that set the stage for something special. When they open, they reveal layers of double petals like petticoats, rosy on the periphery of the flower and fading to a pretty lavender-lilac at the center.

The shrub itself is reasonably compact and somewhat upright, coming into flower rather later than the average French lilac. Use it as a screening plant, as an elegant hedge or at its ornamental best in the border.

Paul Thirion was granted an RHS Award of Garden Merit in 1927 and again in 1969.

....

Syringa vulgaris 'Paul Thirion'
Height 10–13 ft
Spread 10–13 ft
Flower size Large
Scent Lightly fragrant
Color Deep reddish-pink
Foliage A peaceful green foil to the frothy flowers
In the garden An excellent grower
As a cut flower The two-tone double flowers are lavish and luxurious

Souvenir d'Alice Harding

Widely considered one of the best double lilacs available, Souvenir d'Alice Harding boasts a bloom of magnificent substance, with thick, richly layered white petals and full, frothy inflorescences.

Introduced in the 1930s by Victor Lemoine, it commemorates Alice Harding from New Jersey in the USA. Amongst other things, doubtless, she was a peony expert – and Victor dabbled in peonies towards the end of his career. She was also an horticultural writer, and she was sufficiently esteemed in the community that when she visited France, in 1938, she chose an iris at the renowned Cayeux nursery to be named for her as well.

History is silent on whether she ever saw her lilac, but it is a thing of beauty and it does her proud.

Syringa vulgaris 'Souvenir d'Alice Harding'
Height 10–16 ft
Spread 6½–10 ft
Flower size Large
Scent Delicious
Colour Fresh white
Foliage Lush and green
In the garden A fragrant snowstorm
As a cut flower Elegant and magnificent

Nadezhda
syn. Hope

One of several lavish and spectacular flowers bred by the Russian lilac hybridizer Leonid Kolesnikov, Nadezhda is translated as 'Hope', so he was clearly a man who had poetry in his soul.

Designed to provide a longer-lasting than usual display, Nadezhda bears large and prolific panicles of showy blooms. The buds are a rich mauve and open to reveal softly untidy, double flowers in a lighter shade of blue-violet that creates an attractive two-tone effect.

Resistant to disease and easy to grow, this variety does best in full sun. It is upright and has a multi-stemmed habit, which makes it an excellent screening plant, landscape shrub or mixed-border companion. In English, the rather poignant name fits the flower for all sorts of optimistic symbolic gestures.

....

Syringa vulgaris 'Nadezhda' syn. 'Hope'
Height 8–10 ft
Spread 5–6½ ft
Flower size Large
Scent Intense
Color Blue-violet
Foliage Fresh green
In the garden Adaptable and striking
As a cut flower Delightful

Rustica

Fancy, frilly and really rather charming, Rustica is more pink than true lilac – dabbling with purple when in bud but then eschewing the darker hues. As the double flowers open, they transmogrify, running through stages of shell pink, baby pink and candyfloss, until they are almost white, with just a touch of violet.

This lilac is naturally beautiful in the garden, but it really excels when brought indoors and displayed in a vase, where the subtle complexities of the flowers can be studied and the exquisite fragrance enjoyed.

Syringa vulgaris 'Rustica'
Height Up to 10 ft
Spread Up to 8 ft
Flower size Large
Scent Sweetly sumptuous
Color A rainbow in pale pink
Foliage Green and somewhat heart-shaped
In the garden A charming and frothy addition
As a cut flower A detailed and enjoyable centerpiece

Madame Charles Souchet

Glamorous, glorious and liberally produced, the flowers of Madame Charles Souchet are a truly beautiful shade of blue. Not cerulean, exactly, more the color of a crepuscular winter sky. That depth of hue you get as evening starts to fall; when the sun is gone, the stars are yet to emerge and the heavens are clear, pink-tinged indigo.

In the garden, it is a plant of outstanding substance and quality, but the showy flowers really come into their own when harvested by the armful, conditioned overnight, then piled into a vase where they can take pride of place in an interior scheme, or be combined with other blooms according to taste.

The lavender buds nestling among the open flowers enhance the gorgeous indigo-blue effect and it is a combination that would look lovely with white or pink blossom, to evoke spring awakenings, or arranged with white and purple tulips for something cooler and more sophisticated.

Bred by the Lemoine Nursery and introduced in 1949, there is a suggestion that it may have a hint of ×*hyacinthiflora* in its makeup, due to its early May flowering time.

....

Syringa vulgaris 'Madame Charles Souchet'
Height Up to 10 ft
Spread Up to 8 ft
Flower size Large
Scent Heady
Color Pale indigo and lavender
Foliage Fresh green
In the garden Easy to grow
As a cut flower Beautiful in a bouquet for any occasion

Victor Lemoine

While Victor Lemoine's name has become synonymous with lilacs, people sometimes forget that he was an accomplished horticulturist who racked up many other achievements over the course of a distinguished career.

Just before his thirtieth birthday he was mentioned in the *Revue Horticole* in relation to a new *Portulaca* he'd bred, and he went on to experiment with *Potentilla*, *Fuchsia*, *Pelargonium* and *Weigela*. In fact, it was nearly another 20 years before he got around to *Syringa* – and, even then, he continued to develop other garden plants, including *Spirea*, *Canna*, saxifrages and peonies. In the fullness of time, he was awarded the Veitch Memorial Medal by the RHS, together with the George R. White Medal of Honor by the Massachusetts Horticultural Society.

The lilac that bears his name is suitably mighty, handsome and upright with flowers that are charming and unostentatious. It is, in fact, entirely appropriate for the man who bred so many.

Syringa vulgaris 'Victor Lemoine'
Height Up to 23 ft
Spread Up to 16 ft
Flower size Large
Scent Classic lilac
Color Deep lilac in a minor key
Foliage Lush
In the garden Makes a fine specimen
As a cut flower Beautiful combined with paler shades of purple and with white

Michel Buchner

If what you want is a large lilac with impressive garden impact you could do a lot worse than Michel Buchner.

A tall variety that is characteristically easy to grow, it has substantial leaves and a profusion of pale mauve flowers, clustered into panicles that look for all the world like large, showy feather dusters. The perfume is delicious and intense; the flowers cut well, and they will have even greater impact when brought indoors and massed in a bucket or large vase.

Grow as a large multi-stemmed shrub or small tree, pruning back superfluous lower branches to reveal its structure and enable other plants to thrive nearby.

Syringa vulgaris 'Michel Buchner'
Height 13–20 ft
Spread 8–10 ft
Flower size Large
Scent Powerfully perfumed
Color Clear mauve
Foliage Medium-green and heart-shaped
In the garden Makes an attractive small tree
As a cut flower Superb

Émile Lemoine

Émile Lemoine's lilac legacy is remarkable and it is no surprise that there is a particularly fabulous variety that bears his name. Indeed, the eponymous plant is a real beauty, a frothy, floriferous double with two-tone flowers that look rather like each floret is kicking up its purple and blue underskirts.

Having helped his father since childhood, Émile Lemoine lived his whole life for lilacs and presided over the introduction of a huge number of lilac cultivars. As gardening luminaries rather than administrative geniuses, their record keeping was almost inevitably somewhat scanty and, as a result, it is impossible to distinguish the overlapping work of Lemoine *père* and Lemoine *fils*, but there were undoubtedly collaborations.

It seems likely that Émile had a hand in many of the 64 outstanding lilac cultivars that were released between 1900 and 1911, the year of Victor Lemoine's death, aged 89. And over the following 20 years, he went on to launch another 62 new lilacs, which were clearly all his own work.

Syringa vulgaris 'Émile Lemoine'
Height 10 ft
Spread 10 ft
Flower size Medium to large
Scent Nicely scented
Color Lilac and powder blue
Foliage Bluish-green
In the garden A hardy upright shrub, which tends to sucker
As a cut flower Team with airy, frothy umbels and lots of foliage

Charles Joly

Packing a perfumed punch and with flowers of a retina-searing shade of magenta, this lilac makes its presence felt.

Charles Joly arrived on the garden scene in 1896, via the work of the Lemoine Nursery, and it has been a firm favorite ever since. Usually grown as a small and bushy tree or a large, rounded shrub, it is a versatile plant, tolerant of drought and disease, and which can be kept in check with judicious pruning.

The conical flower heads are smaller than many of the newer varieties, but due to the dramatic color and all-round good nature it is considered one of the best double purples available.

Syringa vulgaris 'Charles Joly'
Height Up to 13 ft
Spread Up to 13 ft
Flower size Medium
Scent Very fragrant
Color Bright magenta
Foliage Mid-green
In the garden A good, reliable plant
As a cut flower The modest-sized flower heads work well when combined with other seasonal flowers, such as tulips, apple blossom and aquilegia

Souvenir de L. Thibault

Lilacs, it seems, have an almost magical quality; one whiff of the bloom can transport a person back in time, to places they have not been and people they have not seen, perhaps for many a year.

In many paeans to this distinctive flower nostalgia is a common theme, and judging by the number of lilacs that are named in memory of someone loved, eminent or special, perhaps it ever was so.

In addition to Souvenir de Louis Thibault, we have Souvenir d'Alice Harding (page 46), named to honor the American garden writer and grande dame of peonies, and Souvenir de Georges Truffaut, for the notable French research scientist who specialized in horticulture. From Germany, we have Andenken an Ludwig Späth, after the eponymous proprietor of a notable nursery, and named by his son.

Depending on where the lilacs are growing, these may be translated backwards and forwards, so outside Germany you sometimes find Andenken an Ludwig Späth as Souvenir de Louis Spaeth, or even just Louis Spaeth, yet the sentiment is apposite, still.

....

Syringa vulgaris 'Souvenir de L. Thibaut' aka 'Souvenir de Louis Thibault'
Height Up to 10 ft
Spread Up 8 ft
Flower size Medium to large
Scent Rather lovely
Color Rose-mauve
Foliage Green and heart-shaped
In the garden Performs well
As a cut flower The soft, adaptable color works well as part of almost any interior scheme

Le Nôtre

This beautiful double lilac arrived on the scene in 1922 and does not look like it is going anywhere soon. The highly double flowers are uniquely colored among lilacs, with a tight, grayish central boss surrounded by cupped outer petals that are an indecisive but attractive pinkish-purple, and smoke-gray on the reverse.

The plant is named for the legendary André le Nôtre, who was landscape gardener to Louis XIV and designed the garden at the Palace of Versailles, taking it from a muddy swamp to the pinnacle of French formal garden design.

....

Syringa vulgaris 'Le Nôtre'
Height 10–13 ft
Spread Up to 8 ft
Flower size Medium
Scent Deliciously perfumed
Color Purple, pink and gray
Foliage Mid-green
In the garden A good, reliable plant
As a cut flower Astonishing and eye-catching, a real talking point that holds its own in a vase

Rosace

This pretty lilac opens in phases, producing a bicolor effect that is really rather attractive, with clusters of uneven, dark magenta buds that are scattered among the lavender double flowers like rosettes stitched onto a ruched taffeta party frock.

In French, *rosace* actually means rosette, and the lilac itself is an old variety but a good one. It is not very easy to find, but if you do, it'll be a sure-fire winner.

Syringa vulgaris 'Rosace'
Height Up to 10 ft
Spread Around 8 ft
Flower size Large
Scent Sweet, strong lilac perfume
Color Bold pops of magenta on a blue-lilac background
Foliage Faded emerald
In the garden Epitomizes all the glories of spring
As a cut flower The belle of the ball

Comte de Kerchove

The de Kerchoves of Denterghem are an ancient and aristocratic Belgian family, and while they have distinguished themselves as landowners and politicians for centuries, they all, almost without exception, love plants.

In the late nineteenth century, the family transformed an area around their castle in Ghent into an extensive park, but it was Oswald, third Count de Kerchove de Denterghem (1844–1906) who perhaps made the greatest mark.

Like his forebears he pursued politics and law, but he was a botanist at heart, and he was also a prolific writer of articles and produced several books on such exotica as palms and orchids. It does not seem far-fetched, then, that the fascinated peer and the expert nurseryman should cross paths and even exchange ideas and horticultural gossip, much as is the case today.

The family were influential in gardening circles, and since 1875 have almost continuously held the presidency of the Royal Society for Agriculture and Botany. By 1899, one of the Comtes de Kerchove had made sufficient an impression on Monsieur Lemoine senior to be honored in lilac immortality, and a very handsome plant it is, too.

Syringa vulgaris 'Comte de Kerchove'
Height 8–12 ft
Spread 8–12 ft
Flower size Medium
Scent Lovely
Color Painterly tones of magenta and lavender
Foliage Unremarkable green
In the garden An aristocratic addition
As a cut flower Cuts a rather elegant dash

Général Pershing

Dating from the 1920s, lilac Général Pershing was named after the US Army officer John Joseph Pershing, who served on the Western Front in the First World War. This area of intense fighting was close to Nancy and to the Lemoine family's nursery and they naturally took a dim view of German occupation.

So when General "Black Jack" Pershing stormed into the nearby Argonne region with around 600,000 American soldiers, this would have been considered a promising turn of events. The Americans fought alongside the French in a sustained offensive that contributed to Germany calling for an armistice. Although Pershing was criticized for his tactics, which were thought to have cost American lives, he was decorated as a hero – and he must have seemed as such to the liberated French lilac-growers.

Left to his own devices, Pershing would have pushed back to occupy and crush Germany, and one doesn't get the impression that his was a flowers-in-gun-barrels style, but despite being named after such a divisive and pugilistic military character, the flower is very beautiful and would grace any home or garden.

Syringa vulgaris 'Général Pershing'
Height 6½–10 ft
Spread 3–5 ft
Flower size Medium
Scent Very fragrant
Color A symphony of lavender and white
Foliage Light green
In the garden A compact plant, good for a smaller garden
As a cut flower Simply beautiful

Cool
Perfection

President Lincoln

This bluest of lilacs was named to honor the 16th American President, who guided the country through the American Civil War in which the victory of the North led to the abolition of slavery. But though Lincoln united the disparate factions, and is remembered as a hero, he was assassinated by a Confederate sympathizer in April 1865, while at the theatre.

Later that year Walt Whitman wrote a long poem of memorial, in which he used pastoral imagery to convey grief; describing the fading light of a falling star, the crying out of nature and the gradual acceptance of death. The flowers and scent of lilac are used in some sections to explore the cycle of life and represent succor for the soul.

In the dooryard fronting an old farm-house near the white-wash'd palings,
Stands the lilac-bush tall-growing with heart-shaped leaves of rich green,
With many a pointed blossom rising delicate, with the perfume strong I love,
With every leaf a miracle – and from this bush in the dooryard,
With delicate-color'd blossoms and heart-shaped leaves of rich green,
A sprig with its flower I break.

The imagery appears again later in the poem:

With the tolling tolling bells' perpetual clang,
Here, coffin that slowly passes,
I give you my sprig of lilac.

'When Lilacs Last in the Dooryard Bloom'd' – Walt Whitman

....

Syringa vulgaris 'President Lincoln'
Height 10 ft
Spread 6½ ft
Flower size Medium
Scent A trip down memory lane
Color Beautiful blue
Foliage Produces lashings of leaves
In the garden A reliable and fast-growing shrub with an erect habit
As a cut flower Resembles a bunch of sky

Lilac Sunday

Compared to the heritage lilacs that make their presence felt in parks and gardens across the nation, in some cases well over 100 years after they first appeared, Lilac Sunday is a new kid on the block. But even though it is a youngster, it has made quite an impression.

Its arrival was a bit of a surprise, however. The story goes that in 1978, John Alexander III, plant propagator at the Arnold Arboretum of Harvard University, Boston, USA, acquired some lilac seeds from the Institute of Botany at the Chinese Academy of Sciences in Beijing, as part of an exchange of knowledge between the two countries. They were planted – with some excitement, one might imagine – and soon they began to grow.

After a while, John observed something unusual: one plant was different; strange and exciting.

It was peculiarly, charmingly willowy, with a delicate shape and arching branches, and the form of the flowers astonished and appealed in equal measure. For rather than one conical panicle at the end of each branch, like most lilacs, this prodigy produced small clusters all along the stem, creating the effect of a giant, cascading, single inflorescence, s 24 inches long.

Winning over all who saw it, the beautiful and floriferous new plant was formally introduced in 1997 and named Lilac Sunday after the Arboretum's signature event, held every year on Mother's Day, which is in early May in the USA.

....

Syringa × chinensis 'Lilac Sunday'
Height 10–15 ft
Spread 10–15 ft
Flower size Medium
Scent Fragrant
Color Lavender-pink
Foliage Pointed, deep green leaves
In the garden An elegant specimen
As a cut flower Use on its own or to add a soft froth of mauve to a mixed arrangement

Maréchal Foch

By the 1920s, Émile Lemoine was developing quite a habit of naming his plants after military types, particularly those who had, from his perspective, saved the day by distinguishing themselves around Nancy during the First World War, and Maréchal Foch is one of these.

The lilac is named for Marshal Ferdinand Foch, who does not appear to have been a particularly moderate man, but he was a successful pugilist and military strategist. Over the course of the war he supervised a number of successful offensives – and a few disasters – and coordinated the efforts of the British, French and Americans, eventually becoming the Supreme Commander of the Allied Armies.

Historically, he is divisive, and in some quarters it is felt that his reckless decisions caused unnecessary loss of life, but he is sufficiently prominent and well-regarded in France that there is also a red grape cultivar named after him.

The eponymous lilac was introduced in 1924. The magenta-pink buds open into large, paler purple florets with slightly cupped or reflexed petals, which fade gradually to lavender.

Lilac Maréchal Foch received an Award of Garden Merit in 1935.

....

Syringa vulgaris 'Maréchal Foch'
Height 10–13 ft
Spread Around 8 ft
Flower size Medium
Scent Evocative and timeless
Color A delicate symphony of purples
Foliage Somewhat heart-shaped and a pleasant shade of green
In the garden A fighting force
As a cut flower White floral companions and silver foliage will pick up the highlights on the delicate, curled lilac flowers

Henri Martin

The Arnold Arboretum of Harvard University, Boston, USA has an extensive collection of lilacs, and in the early 1980s a study was carried out in which volunteer "sniffologists" assigned a scent rating to 456 samples, and Henri Martin rated very highly.

Scent is a science in itself; the perfume of any flower, be it a magnolia, a rose or a lilac, is made up of many different chemical compounds and can be affected by various factors, including the temperature and the age of the bloom. And while perception of scent is highly subjective, it led to erudite ponderings on the matter, and even the suggestion that the fragrance of any particular cultivar can vary in quality and intensity from year to year, rather like wine.

But if perfume is what you are after, Henri Martin is a very fine choice. It is a Lemoine selection and was named in honor of the nineteenth-century historian and politician, who compiled a notable 15-volume *Histoire de France*.

Syringa vulgaris 'Henri Martin'
Height Up to 10 ft
Spread Up to 8 ft
Flower size Large
Scent Top class
Color Smoky mauve
Foliage Dull green
In the garden Impressively frothy
As a cut flower Beautiful, if you have a vase large enough

Jeanne d'Arc

The story of Jeanne d'Arc – or Joan of Arc – the Maid of Orléans, is legendary. Born in around 1412, the daughter of a peasant farmer, she started hearing divine voices in her early teens. These determined her mission: she should fight to expel the English from France and return the rightful French king to his throne.

Defying her father's attempts to marry her off, she took a vow of chastity and made her way to Chinon, where she talked her way into an audience with the disinherited Prince Charles de Valois and promised him that she would see him crowned king at Reims.

Dressed in white armor and riding a white horse, she secured valiant victories against the Anglo-Burgundy forces, breaking the siege of Orléans and driving her opponents across the River Loire. King Charles II was crowned, but the wavering monarch was advised that Joan was becoming too powerful, and when she was captured by the enemy and tried on charges of heresy, witchcraft and dressing like a man, he did nothing to save her.

Joan of Arc was burned at the stake in the marketplace at Rouen, aged 19, but just 20 years later a new trial ordered by Charles VII cleared her name. She has since become one of the most popular saints in history and was canonized by Pope Benedict XV in 1920.

A symbol of French unity and nationalism, she is commemorated by a double white lilac.

....

Syringa vulgaris 'Jeanne d'Arc'
Height Up to 10 ft
Spread Up to 8 ft
Flower size Medium
Scent Beautiful fragrance
Color Virginal white
Foliage Pointed, green and a pleasant contrast to the white flowers
In the garden A good, reliable plant
As a cut flower Simple and demure in a single-variety arrangement

Arch McKean

Introduced by American hybridizer Reverend John Fiala in 1984 from his cross between *Syringa* classics Agincourt Beauty (page 189) and Rochester, and honoring the eponymous Michigan lilac specialist, Arch McKean is thoroughly glorious.

The mature plant will make a substantial landscape specimen, is vigorous enough to hold its own in a shrub border and, with no great tendency to sucker, it also won't overwhelm its neighbors in a more herbaceous setting.

The flowers are large and showy, each chunky single floret a beautiful clear purple that intensifies to indigo in the center. Densely packed enough for drama and impact, but loose enough that each one can be appreciated for its own merits, the overall effect is really rather ravishing.

Syringa vulgaris 'Arch McKean'
Height 8 ft
Spread 9 ft
Flower size Large
Scent Powerfully fragrant
Color Clear magenta-purple with a touch of indigo
Foliage Blue-green
In the garden A handsome back-of-the-border shrub
As a cut flower Classically elegant

Président Grévy

This magnificent and well-loved lilac was named after François Paul Jules Grévy, who was President of France from 1879–87. And, like many plants that have stood the test of time, it has become a treasured garden staple.

The immense panicles of flowers are made up of tightly clustered double flowers in a delicious shade of baby blue, made warmer and more sophisticated by the heliotrope color of the unopened buds.

A vigorous, reliable and well-formed plant, Président Grévy is a good specimen shrub and works well as part of a mixed border, too. Alternatively, try cutting an armful of long stems and arrange the confection of flowers and leaves in a heavy-bottomed vase.

Syringa vulgaris 'Président Grévy'
Height 6½–13 ft
Spread 5–6½ ft
Flower size Very large
Scent Highly fragrant
Color Lilac-blue
Foliage Light-green, heart-shaped leaves
In the garden A good foundation shrub with a spectacular spring display
As a cut flower Bold and striking

Edward J. Gardner

Appearing regularly on lists of the very best pink lilacs around, Edward J. Gardner is highly esteemed indeed.

The double flowers are very open, flared and flattened in such a way that it manages to look neat and elegant, rather than in any way bunched or untidy, as some of its many-petaled brethren can.

Easy to grow and relatively compact, this lilac is a fine addition to a collection or a border, filling the air with sweet perfume and muddling in nicely with surrounding flowers and foliage.

Edward J. Gardner holds an Award of Garden Merit from the Royal Horticultural Society and is marketed as Flamingo™ in Germany.

Syringa vulgaris 'Edward J. Gardner'
Height 8–10 ft
Spread 6–8 ft
Flower size Medium to large
Scent Wonderful
Color Smoky lavender-pink
Foliage Green
In the garden A good, reliable plant
As a cut flower The subtle color and tousled blooms mix well with a range of other flowers

Pocahontas

Like other lilacs bred by Canadian hybridizer Frank Skinner, Pocahontas is supremely hardy and, since it flowers joyfully in late spring – a good two weeks earlier than varieties of *Syringa vulgaris* – it can be used to bring forward the lilac season.

The shrub is moderate in size and the foliage emerges bronze before darkening to a green summer livery. The upright panicles are a mass of small, rather waxy flowers; maroon in bud, these become a refined shade of violet upon opening, and are rather reminiscent of blackberry cream.

Beautiful and rather dramatic, this flower is named for the Native American princess who, thanks to the power of her legend, has become a household name. Born in the late sixteenth century, Pocahontas became an influential link with the Christian colonialists before her death in London in her early twenties. It is a story that has become romanticized and embellished over the centuries, even fabricated in parts, but there seems little doubt that she was a brave, lively, clever and resourceful young woman, and her lilac flower is similarly captivating.

....

Syringa ×hyacinthiflora 'Pocahontas'
Height 6½–8 ft
Spread 6½–8 ft
Flower size Small
Scent Delicate
Color Rich violet-purple
Foliage Healthy and mid-green
In the garden Use matching plants either side of a gateway or try weaving through with early-flowering clematis in a harmonious color scheme
As a cut flower Try combining with white or purple alliums and the evergreen twigs of herbs such as rosemary or sage

Adelaide Dunbar

When John Dunbar became Assistant Superintendent of Parks at Rochester, New York, he went quietly mad for lilacs. In 1891, in a move that would make the plant and the place synonymous for lilac-lovers worldwide, he planted around 100 French Hybrid lilacs at Highland Botanical Park, and the site promptly became a place of pilgrimage for *Syringa* fanciers, far and wide.

But Dunbar was not yet done. Through the action of bees, butterflies and a thousand other pollinating insects, the cultivars of original planting yielded hybrids of their own. Some of these open-pollinated seedlings he collected and grew on, and Adelaide Dunbar was introduced in 1916.

Fairly upright and compact, this slightly leggy plant has become a garden favorite, despite some tendency to suckering, and is usually grown as a multi-stemmed shrub. Perfumed, intensely purple panicles are produced in peak lilac season and it is a breathtaking sight in full spate.

Syringa vulgaris 'Adelaide Dunbar'
Height 12 ft
Spread 10 ft
Flower size Medium
Scent Deliciously fragrant
Color Magenta-violet
Foliage Green, heart-shaped leaves
In the garden A useful splash of spring interest
As a cut flower A strong color and vintage looks make this a classic

Prodige

Epitomizing all that is good and beautiful about lilacs, Prodige will fit seamlessly into almost any spring planting scheme. The color is a clear, glorious purple; not so dark as to vanish into the gloom, and not uncomfortably light either, and the wide, single flowers are borne in lavish and dramatic panicles.

Provide this paragon with a prime spot in the garden, where it can be seen from the windows or doors – and smelled, too. Surround it with complementary companions for a floral spring-to-summer vista, including shrubs and small trees such as Weigela, Philadelphus or flowering crab apples, with perhaps irises, honeysuckle and roses to continue the display.

Syringa vulgaris 'Prodige'
Height Up to 10 ft
Spread Up to 6½ ft
Flower size Medium to large
Scent Very fine
Color A sweetly juicy violet
Foliage Green
In the garden Prodige has considerable impact in the spring border
As a cut flower A vision of nostalgia

Lavender Lady

During the early twentieth century in the USA, lilacs were loved and lauded. This was a plant rich in old-world charm that was welcome in backyards and landscapes across the continent. Yet there were some would-be lilac growers who were doomed to disappointment.

For, while there had been great success in making this hardy shrub even hardier, to accommodate the chilly north, the intransigent *Syringa*, far from its cool native home, turned its nose up at the prospect of steamy southern gardens. They might just about grow, but most lilacs, including *S. vulgaris* and "the other sort of *S. ×hyacinthiflora* cultivars" (hybrids of *S. oblata* subsp. *oblata* × *S. vulgaris*), require a proper dose of cold weather to flower properly the following spring.

But in the early 1950s, a California-based gentleman called Walter Edward Lammerts released his new lilac, 'Lavender Lady' into the nursery trade. This particular *×hyacinthiflora* hybrid was a rebel with a rock 'n' roll approach to temperature. She shrugged in the face of warm winters, and with proven success, Lammerts went on to breed a number of other mild-winter cultivars, including Heather Haze and Sweet Charity, while Angel White (page 129) was introduced in 1971.

Lammerts later received an International Lilac Society Award of Merit for his pioneering work in introducing new cultivars for southern areas.

Still available today, Lavender Lady is a gorgeous creature, with petals that curl right back to reveal a splash of cerulean blue at the very center of the flower.

....

Syringa ×hyacinthiflora 'Lavender Lady'
Height 16 ft
Spread 16 ft
Flower size Medium to large
Scent Sweet and intoxicating
Color Pale lilac with a blue heart
Foliage Mid-blue-green
In the garden Wonderfully floriferous and tolerant of warm winters
As a cut flower Absolutely captivating

Pasteur

One of the most eminent scientists of the nineteenth century, Louis Pasteur is credited with the discoveries of microbial fermentation and pasteurization, the development of germ theory and the development of vaccines for anthrax and rabies. He also established the Pasteur Institute, in 1887.

He is frequently quoted as saying, *"Dans les champs de l'observation, le hasard ne favorise que les esprits préparés."* This translates as, "In the field of observation, chance favors only the prepared mind."

Gardeners and nursery folk are very familiar with this. Chance, observation and preparedness is, after all, what brings many great plants into cultivation. And perhaps Victor and Émile Lemoine had this motto in the back of their minds, as they looked over their new batch of seedling lilacs, around the turn of the last century.

In any case, the plant they picked to honor the great man is lovely indeed, with simple, single, cupped flowers in a shade of raven purple that is both subtle and exquisite.

Syringa vulgaris 'Pasteur'
Height 10–13 ft
Spread Around 8 ft
Flower size Medium
Scent Delightful
Color Inky purple
Foliage A pleasant shade of green
In the garden Well-behaved and reliable
As a cut flower A really beautiful addition to a scheme with a deep purple emphasis, and a fittingly sombre hue for funeral flowers

Delicate Delights

Esther Staley

The original *Syringa* ×*hyacinthiflora* hybrids were developed in France in the 1870s by the Lemoine family and someone, somewhere along the line, decided that the inflorescence looked a bit like a hyacinth, whence came the name. And, since it's impossible to have too much of a good thing, people have been improving on them ever since.

Esther Staley was introduced by Walter Bosworth Clarke in 1948. Responsible for a number of excellent plants, Walter was heavily involved in developing early flowering lilacs and warm-winter hybrids, of which Esther Staley is one.

Tall and elegant, the substantial panicles are made up of magenta-plum buds that open to reveal bright lilac flowers that are somewhat lighter towards the center of the bloom. The Esther Staley for whom this plant is named was an outstanding gardener, based in California.

Esther Staley was granted an Award of Garden Merit by the RHS in 1961 and 1993.

Syringa ×*hyacinthiflora* 'Esther Staley'
Height Up to 13 ft
Spread 8 ft
Flower size Medium to large
Scent Strongly fragrant
Color Vibrant purple
Foliage Heart-shaped, emerges bronze and develops to green
In the garden Easy to grow and lovely to look at
As a cut flower Absolutely gorgeous

Syringa × chinensis 'Bicolor'

The lilac variety *Syringa × chinensis* 'Bicolor' arose rather later than its esteemed parent. The story goes that, around 1850, Victor Lemoine was visiting a private garden when, on one particular lilac, he noticed a branch-sport: a part of the plant that has mutated in such a way that it is visually different to the rest.

It looked promising so, good nurseryman that he was, he took a cutting, rooted it up and grew it on. And *Syringa × chinensis* 'Bicolor' is a beauty. The flowers are exquisite, small, single and white in color, with an intense amethyst mark at the throat and corollas tinted the same hue. The shrub, meanwhile, is large and forms a good garden backdrop.

Syringa × chinensis 'Bicolor'
Height Around 10 ft
Spread Around 8 ft
Flower size Small
Scent Gently fragrant
Color Slate-wash with violet highlights
Foliage Simple and green
In the garden Resembles a fluffy lavender cloud
As a cut flower Delicate and airy

Prophecy

The species lilac *Syringa yunnanensis* is not well-known, but it is a useful sort of plant. More of a small tree than a shrub, the slim, pale flowers are produced late in the season and, while it roots well from cuttings, it tends not to sucker.

Prophecy arose as part of a number of experiments conducted by John Fiala in the mid-twentieth century, in which he sought to alter the chromosomes of lilac plants, and thus generate new varieties. He did this by dipping seedlings in a toxic, mutagenic solution of colchicine, and *Syringa yunnanensis* – now *S. tomentella* subsp. *yunnanensis* – was one of the varieties of lilac he chose as experimental material.

While the mortality rate in seedlings treated this way is very high, some usually survive, and in 1969 Fiala introduced the slow-growing cultivar Prophecy.

Prophecy has flowers that are larger than its parents and which are deeper in hue.

....

Syringa tomentella subsp. *yunnanensis* 'Prophecy'
Height 10–16 ft
Spread 6½–12 ft
Flower size Variable
Scent Fragrant
Color Baby mauve
Foliage Dull green
In the garden Makes an attractive floral hedge
As a cut flower Less dominant than many lilacs, Prophecy is pretty in a small, mixed posy

Syringa × laciniata

Referred to sometimes as the cut-leafed lilac, *Syringa × laciniata* was once believed to be a botanical variety of *S. persica*, then considered to be a species rather than a hybrid. It is now, however, thought to be a cross between *Syringa protolaciniata* and another, unknown, parent, but its place of origin, and the means by which it entered cultivation, remain a tantalizing mystery.

Yet it is a good and solid garden plant. Rather than being smooth, the leaves are incised or feathered along the margins, which provides an attractive additional detail after the flowers are gone. It is also reasonably tolerant of heat and resistant to mildew, while the willowy, arched quality of the branches gives it a fine appearance.

In older literature, this lilac is sometimes still referred to as *Syringa × persica* var. *laciniata* or *S. × persica laciniata*.

Syringa × laciniata
Height 12 ft
Spread 12 ft
Flower size Fairly small
Scent Pleasant
Color Soft lavender
Foliage Not large, and middling green in color but more interesting in form than average
In the garden Lends itself to a smaller garden
As a cut flower Cut long branches for an airy display

Angel White
syn. White Angel

A vision of seraphic beauty and purity, Angel White was bred by Walter Edward Lammerts in the latter half of the twentieth century.

Lilacs had become well-established in America, and although they were much loved, their liking for cool winters made them frustratingly unsuitable for the hot and sometimes humid southern states. But all this changed when Lammerts released heat-tolerant Lavender Lady (page 113) in 1954 and he went on to breed several more "warm-winter" lilacs, including Angel White, which was introduced in 1971.

Angel White is a tall and airy shrub with slightly drooping panicles about 8 inches long. While bred to grace gardens in mild-winter areas, it may prove itself increasingly important to gardeners in regions that are presently marginal for conventional lilacs and may become hotter still as the climate changes. Angel White is a versatile garden shrub and the flowers are elegant and stylish in a vase.

. . . .

Syringa ×hyacinthiflora 'Angel White', syn. 'White Angel'
Height Up to 13 ft
Spread Up to 10 ft
Flower size Medium
Scent Delightfully fragrant
Color Pure white
Foliage Cool sage green
In the garden Ideal for warmer areas and those that become marginal due to climate change
As a cut flower Recommended

Syringa josikaea

Native to mountainous areas of Central and Eastern Europe, *Syringa josikaea*, or the Hungarian lilac as it is sometimes known, is a moderately sized shrub that is now considered endangered in the wild.

Brought into cultivation in the early nineteenth century, it had originally been spotted by Hungarian botanist Pál Kitaibel, but his botanical description of the plant left a lot to be desired, so in the end it was named for Rosalia, Baroness von Josika, née Countess Czaky, who collected plants and sent them to the Imperial and Royal University in Vienna, where it was first officially described.

In cultivation, *Syringa josikaea* has hybridized with *S. komarowii*, to which it is closely related, and the resulting offspring is known as *S. × josiflexa*.

Syringa josikaea is often used as the rootstock for grafted lilacs.

....

Syringa josikaea
Height 12 ft
Spread 12 ft
Flower size Small to medium
Scent Sweetly and strongly perfumed
Color Perfectly lilac
Foliage Smallish, rather pointed leaves
In the garden A hardy and spreading plant
As a cut flower Pretty and dainty

Miss Canada

Hot pink and super-sassy, Miss Canada is a cheerleader among late-flowering lilacs and she is the work of William Cumming, who was the brother-in-law of Frank Skinner, legendary breeder of a fine range of cold-tolerant plants.

Flowering several weeks after the main gamut of *Syringa vulgaris*, Miss Canada is the progeny of *S.* × *josiflexa* 'Redwine' and *S.* × *prestoniae* 'Hiawatha', and while she is sometimes classed as an × *prestoniae* lilac, in fact this plant is within the Villosae Group.

Lilac Miss Canada is compact and relatively slow-growing, which makes it ideal for smaller gardens. The small, tubular flowers are sweetly scented, and bubblegum-pink buds open to reveal paler pink single blooms, the interiors of which are the shade of strawberry ice cream.

....

Syringa Villosae Group 'Miss Canada'
Height 6–10 ft
Spread 6–10 ft
Flower size Medium
Scent Sweet
Color Rose pink and baby pink
Foliage Green
In the garden A cheerful splash of color, especially when paired with peonies and campanula
As a cut flower Makes a pretty posy for a smaller vase

Syringa × chinensis

The perverse thing about *Syringa × chinensis*, is that it is not, in fact, from China. It emerged in the botanical garden at Rouen in France, in the late eighteenth century, most likely as a naturally occurring hybrid between *S. laciniata* and *S. vulgaris* – at least, this was the opinion of Émile Lemoine, who performed large numbers of similar crosses in the course of his breeding work.

Back then, however, it was considered a species and was, eventually, described by German botanist Carl Willdenow. This means the suffix "Willd" is sometimes appended to the name, for extra confusion and head-scratching among the uninitiated.

But whatever the shaggy dog story of its name may be, the Rouen lilac is a thing of great beauty. Several trusses of flowers are borne at the end of each branch, creating an arching effect which, despite the small size of the individual florets, has considerable garden impact.

The foliage is attractive in spring but it can be susceptible to powdery mildew in late summer, so consider screening it with tall, late-flowering perennials, such as dahlias, asters or *Verbena bonariensis*. An upright, rounded shrub in its youth, it becomes leggy and more spreading with age, but if the width of the plant is kept in check this provides a good opportunity to underplant with winter flowers.

....

Syringa × chinensis
Height Around 12 ft
Spread Around 8 ft
Flower size Medium
Scent Strong and most attractive
Color Purest deep lilac
Foliage Dull green, smallish and pointed oval in shape
In the garden A beautiful specimen shrub and it makes a good hedge, too
As a cut flower Wonderful as part of a lavish arrangement with white and green flowers, and perhaps a shot of rich plum or bright blue

Albert F. Holden

True bicolor lilacs are few and far between, but many of them dabble with variations in hue and Albert F. Holden is one of these.

Each thyrsus is made up of a cluster of rather irregularly shaped, dark pink buds and these open into wide single flowers with slightly incurved petals. The front of each petal deepens to a richer blue-purple, while to the rear it develops a silvery bloom. The effect is showy and dramatic, and due to the curly quality of some of the flowers, it gives the overall impression of a conical mass of purple popcorn.

Introduced in 1980 by Reverend John Fiala, it is a hybrid of Sarah Sands and Réaumur and was named to honor the founder of the Arnold Arboretum at Harvard University, Boston.

Syringa vulgaris 'Albert F. Holden'
Height 7 ft
Spread 7 ft
Flower size Large
Scent Intensely floral
Color Rich purple with a silver reverse
Foliage Green, heart-shaped leaves
In the garden A good specimen
As a cut flower Team with lighter mauves and silvers to emphasize the two-tone flowers

Syringa × persica

Originally described as a species, and recognized by Linnaeus as such, *Syringa × persica* is a hybrid of uncertain origin and has only ever been known as a cultivated plant.

In 1672, Dutch botanist and physician Abraham Munting referred to it as *Jasminum persicum foliis integris*, while in 1695, Paul Hermann, who was Professor of Botany and Director of the Botanical Garden at the University of Leiden, listed – probably the same plant – *Syringha persica foliis integris*, in what could have been the first use of the name *Syringa*.

But for the purposes of sheer enjoyment of the flower, none of this matters too much; for it is a creature of great beauty. The flowers are starlike, with four sharply pointed petals and a splash of cobalt at the throat. Beautiful enough for any bouquet and compact enough for a smaller garden, it is a plant that is both useful and gorgeous to look at.

Syringa × persica
Height 5 ft
Spread 5 ft
Flower size Small to medium
Scent Pleasantly fragrant
Color Violet-lilac with a splash of cobalt blue
Foliage Dark green and narrowly pointed
In the garden A charming addition to a small garden
As a cut flower Captivating

Mme Antoine Buchner

Some double lilacs can come across as a little over-stuffed. Many-petaled florets crammed into tight panicles, looking like portly officials in ill-fitting array on a feast day parade.

But Mme Antoine Buchner is not one of these. No, she is a beautiful, simple thing. A country girl rather than a courtier. With uncomplicated flowers that are airy and delicate, the soft color of an early summer evening, perhaps with a little mist rising. Perfect, in fact, gathered into a posy, with equally gentle and wild companions – grasses and spring foliage, together with whatever flowers present themselves, for a relaxed and informal display.

Mme Antoine Buchner was accorded an Award of Garden Merit in 2012.

Syringa vulgaris 'Mme Antoine Buchner'
Height 10 ft
Spread 8 ft
Flower size Large
Scent Very fragrant
Color Rose-purple and white
Foliage Green
In the garden Moderately vigorous
As a cut flower Highly ornamental

Josée

Although hybrids of *Syringa vulgaris* are legion, by the latter half of the twentieth century the breeders' palette was expanding to consider the potential for smaller, slower-growing lilacs, of which Josée is one.

Created by Georges Morel, who when he was not breeding lilacs was a plant physiologist, virologist and biochemist, it was a hybrid of *Syringa pubescens* subsp. *microphylla* and *S. pubescens* subsp. *patula*, which he then crossed again with *S. meyeri* – or *S. pubescens* subsp. *pubescens*, as it is now known. It was released by Pépinières Minier of Beaufort-en-Vallée, France, in 1974, under the less-than-poetic official name of MORjos 060F.

The result is a dense, compact shrub which is outstandingly useful in small gardens and diminutive enough to grace a container on a patio or balcony. The flowers, though modest in size, are prolific and sweetly scented and, unusually in lilacs, the plant has a tendency to rebloom several times in a season.

The flowers are a mixture of pink, gray and purple or a light puce color to the exterior, and lighter on the inside, while the foliage is healthy with a good resistance to powdery mildew. All in all, a winner.

···

Syringa vulgaris 'Josée'
Height 5 ft
Spread 5 ft
Flower size Small
Scent Sweet
Color Pink and pale pink
Foliage Small, rounded, mid-green leaves
In the garden A good small-garden subject; will work in a container
As a cut flower Dainty mixed in with other seasonal flowers

Mont Blanc

The name Mont Blanc conjures up an image of magnificence: a sturdy, snow-capped mountain, jutting into a brilliant blue sky, and the freshest and most exhilarating of alpine views.

But superior varieties of garden plant exist. To be sure, it is an old one, introduced in the early twentieth century, but nostalgia and an attachment to heritage should not blind us to the fact that while some early lilacs are, and remain, outstanding, dedicated work by generations of plant breeders has improved significantly on others.

While the flowers of Mont Blanc are pretty and really rather dainty, the shrub itself can be weak and weedy. So if vigor and low-maintenance are priorities, other single white lilacs might be a better bet.

Syringa vulgaris 'Mont Blanc'
Height 8 ft
Spread 8 ft
Flower size Medium
Scent Wonderfully fragrant
Color White as snow
Foliage Lightish green
In the garden Better tucked into a corner than given center stage
As a cut flower Fresh and frothy

Syringa oblata

Sometimes known as the broadleaf lilac, *Syringa oblata* blooms several weeks earlier than *S. vulgaris*, and may even break bud in late April, so as long as there is no frost, it makes a fine start to the lilac season. It also, unusually for a lilac, has good autumn color.

Native to China, it is geographically widespread, found in woods and along roadsides, and also cultivated in the gardens of the region. As discussed earlier, when a species has an extensive range a certain amount of variation is inevitable. It also increases the likelihood of plants ending up in different collections with the same name, but which are not phenotypically identical. What's more, as *Syringa oblata* is embedded in the lineage of the glorious and multifarious ×*hyacinthiflora* hybrids, its horticultural reach is widespread generally.

The plants are typically strong and upright. Vigorous in growth, they soon assume the proportions of a small tree – which is perfect if you are looking for a lawn specimen or accent shrub, especially if you prune the lower branches to reveal a "trunk." In smaller spaces, secateurs should be deployed on a regular basis to keep it in check, or a more compact alternative sought.

Syringa oblata
Height Up to 16 ft
Spread Around 10–13 ft
Flower size Variable
Scent Pleasant
Color Gray-mauve, like dawn over the mountains
Foliage The suffix *oblata* references the shape of the leaves, which, for a lilac, are wide
In the garden A substantial specimen
As a cut flower Exquisitely dainty

Agnes Smith

Dainty Agnes Smith is one of several lilacs bred from a series of plants that was originally created by Isabella Preston, then subsequently re-hybridized at the University of New Hampshire. Technically, the Preston-bred female parent was *S. × josiflexa* 'James Macfarlane', which is rather smaller than the average *S. × prestoniae*, but there is a certain fluidity around the naming, compounded by the fact that Agnes Smith is marketed in Germany as *S. × prestoniae* 'Miss USA'®.

Be this as it may, Agnes Smith is an excellent garden plant. Compact, fairly slow-growing and non-suckering, it lends itself to the smaller garden, as a specimen or ornamental hedge, and it could even be used in a large container. Thanks to its Canadian heritage, it is also extremely hardy, to USDA Zone 2.

It flowers at least two weeks later than the main season of *Syringa vulgaris* and its cultivars, so it is a good choice for extending spring interest in the garden. The pretty, airy flowers are finely tubular with incurved petals, less heavy than many lilacs perhaps, but they still cut well and combine pleasantly with other late spring flowers in a vase.

....

Syringa Villosae Group Agnes Smith, aka *S. × prestoniae* 'Agnes Smith' and
S. × josiflexa 'Agnes Smith'
Height 5 ft
Spread Up to 5 ft
Flower size Fairly small
Scent Sweet
Color White
Foliage Rich green
In the garden A compact and useful shrub, ideal for an exposed or windy spot
As a cut flower Attractively understated

Syringa × chinensis 'Saugeana'

Known for its exquisite fragrance as well as its beauty in the garden, Saugeana is a fairly commonly found cultivar of *Syringa × chinensis* that dates from the early nineteenth century. According to lilac lore, like its parent, it came from Rouen; raised from seed and then named for one Monsieur Saugé, who was the son-in-law of M. Varin, who had identified the original Chinese lilac some 30 years previously.

The deliciously scented flowers are a deeper red-pink than the parent, which means that it is sometimes referred to by the synonym 'Rubra'. It is a very fine plant indeed, forming a loose, open, fairly tall shrub.

Syringa × chinensis 'Saugeana'
Height Up to 15 ft
Spread 8 ft
Flower size Fairly large
Scent One of the most fragrant lilacs there is
Color Deep reddish-pink
Foliage Pleasant green and neatly pointed
In the garden Colorful and attractively lacy
As a cut flower Will scent a room

Syringa pubescens subsp. *microphylla*

syn. *S. microphylla*

This interesting and versatile little lilac is an excellent choice for smaller gardens, as not only is it compact, but it is one of the few *Syringa* that will sometimes produce a second flush of flowers later in the season.

The plant itself is delicate, with small leaves that are resistant to mildew, while the highly scented flowers are used in China to make tea – according to reports from plant explorer Joseph Hers, following his collecting expedition in the 1920s.

Since this variety is naturally dwarf, it lends itself to growing in containers and, after the standard period of winter chill, it could be brought into a cool greenhouse. It is usually a mid-season bloomer, but thus protected it will flower over a month earlier than it usually would, getting lilac time off to a flying and fragrant start.

Syringa pubescens subsp. *microphylla* is sometimes known as the little leaf lilac or the daphne lilac.

....

Syringa pubescens subsp. *microphylla* syn. *S. microphylla*
Height Up to 12 ft
Spread Up to 12 ft
Flower size Small
Scent One of the most fragrant
Color Each floret is palest pink with a rosy throat and corolla
Foliage A small, pointed oval
In the garden Small enough for a pot or other large container
As a cut flower Charming

Maiden's Blush

This delicate, charming flower was developed by Canadian plant breeder Frank Leith Skinner, who was based at Dropmore, Manitoba. Despite being self-taught, he was a pioneering hybridizer and gardener, who introduced over 300 hardy plants, including roses, clematis and lilacs, in the middle of the twentieth century.

Part of Skinner's motivation was borne of frustration that many of the plants that he heard about and wanted to grow were not cold-tolerant enough to thrive at his homestead (later his nursery), located a chilly 400km (250 miles) north-west of Winnipeg. As a result, Maiden's Blush, introduced in 1966, is hardier still than its contemporaries, and it is said to tolerate temperatures as low as those found in USDA Zone 2.

Earlier-blooming than generic French lilacs, Maiden's Blush is a creature of great beauty; deep pink buds opening to fragrant, shapely, apple-blossom blooms.

Syringa ×hyacinthiflora 'Maiden's Blush' has received an Award of Garden Merit from the RHS and is marketed in Germany as Rosenrot.

....

Syringa ×hyacinthiflora 'Maiden's Blush'
Height 6–8 ft
Spread 6–8 ft
Flower size Medium
Scent Fabulous and intoxicating
Color Soft shell pink
Foliage Dense and glossy
In the garden Compact and multi-stemmed, it makes a good hedge or screen
As a cut flower Pretty teamed with white or mauve lilacs, tulips, peonies or alliums, and with glaucous foliage such as eucalyptus

Congo

Dating all the way back to 1896, Congo is a classic French lilac with all the poise, pizzazz and elegance that one would expect from a plant that emerged from the Lemoine stable.

The flowers are rich and heavy. And, as the tight buds open into florets of the most glorious purple, a light but sweetly uplifting fragrance is revealed.

Over time it grows into a substantial bush and, while it will make an attractive specimen, it also lends itself to growing as a hedge or privacy screen. The stormy and rather pendulous flowers are the main show in late spring, while in autumn the leaves color to an attractive bronze, or dark burgundy, giving the plant another season of interest.

Syringa vulgaris 'Congo'
Height Up to 10 ft
Spread Up to 8 ft
Flower size Large
Scent Very fragrant
Color Fulsome purple
Foliage Mid-green coloring to burgundy in autumn
In the garden Old but most excellent
As a cut flower Impactful flowers that will take center stage in a large vase

Sumptuous
Sophistication

Alice Christianson
syn. Alice Christensen, Alice Christenson

This perky double lilac was bred in the early years of the twentieth century by the Lilac Lady of Woodland, Hulda Klager, who started her breeding work aged 41, with just three named Lemoine lilacs, and continued in her mission until her death in 1960, aged 96.

Although she must have produced many lilac seedlings in her career, surprisingly few of her plants were introduced commercially, though she sold many to customers who came in person to her nursery in the 1920s.

The flowers of Alice Christianson are respectably large in size and liberally produced, the florets forming dense clusters in a symphony of lavender-pink and lavender-blue.

There is a shortage of stock lists and inventories from Hulda Klager's earlier work, and her entire garden was destroyed by a catastrophic flood in 1948, so some of her plants are not particularly well-documented. This may be at least some of the reason why the latter part of this lilac's name is variously spelled Christianson, Christensen or Christenson.

....

Syringa vulgaris 'Alice Christianson' syn. 'Alice Christensen', 'Alice Christenson'
Height Up to 10 ft
Spread Up to 8 ft
Flower size Large and heavy
Scent Intensely fragrant
Color Shades of lavender
Foliage Attractively pointed and lushly green
In the garden The substantial flowers make a statement
As a cut flower Arrange loosely in a vase and team with fresh, green foliage

Etna

Bred by the peerless Émile Lemoine and released into the world in 1927, this magnificent lilac is named after Mount Etna, which is the highest active volcano in Italy and has been erupting for at least 2.6 million years.

The Lemoine Nursery was not that close to Italy, but the mountain's significant activity around that time must have made the news on a regular basis, so when presented with a lilac that had large, conical panicles in a distinctive shade of smoldering purple, the volcano perhaps came to mind.

And the name is a good one for anything with impact, including mountains. The eruption of Mount Etna in 475 BCE was spoken of by Ancient Greeks, including Aeschylus and Pindar, and legends soon arose. The mountain, it was believed, held the workshop of blacksmith to the Gods, Hephaestus – who the Romans called Vulcan – and the Cyclops who is sometimes cast as his assistant. Another theory was that the giant Typhon lay underneath, making the earth shake as he rolled over.

Vigorous in growth and with a tendency to sucker, lilac Etna produces a fine shrub covered in handsome flowers and is well worth growing if you can find it.

....

Syringa vulgaris 'Etna'
Height 9 ft
Spread 7 ft
Flower size Large
Scent Pleasant and strong
Color Smoldering maroon
Foliage Green
In the garden Robust and multi-stemmed with a tendency to sucker
As a cut flower A wonderful anchor to an arrangement; mix with oranges, yellows and a little white to recreate an eruption in a vase

Président Poincaré

Politicians in wartime often have a rough ride, and whatever their strategies may be, they are criticized either for weakness and indecisiveness, or for reckless warmongering.

Through the lens of history, it is hard to be sure precisely what anyone might have thought, but it appears that his concerns about the military threat of Germany and the vulnerability of France were sufficient for Président Poincaré to break out some concerted diplomacy during the years before the First World War, moving to maintain the Franco-Russian alliance and build bridges with Britain for a potential alliance in the case of an outbreak of hostilities.

The lilac that was named in his honor is statesmanly enough for any leader, however, with bushy, intensely fragrant panicles of double flowers, in a handsome livery of violet and lavender.

Syringa vulgaris 'Président Poincaré'
Height Up to 10 ft
Spread 6–8 ft
Flower size Large
Scent Intense and delicious
Color Boldly purple
Foliage Medium-green and slightly glossy
In the garden Eye-catching when planted near a terrace or path
As a cut flower Holds its own among the loveliest lilacs there are

Belle de Nancy

A grande dame of the spring garden, Belle de Nancy was introduced by the Lemoine Nursery in 1891 and it is still one of the best, and most widely available, pink varieties in cultivation.

Tightly furled and clustered, the magenta buds lighten as they open, revealing a froth of surprisingly simple double flowers. The hue matures to an adaptable and charming fresh pink-mauve, darker to the edges and fading to almost white at the center of each floret.

A showy and floriferous plant, Belle de Nancy is more compact than many cultivars of *Syringa vulgaris*, lending itself to situations where space is limited but spring drama will be appreciated.

Try growing it as a low screen or hedge, or even in a large container, where it can be underplanted with ferns and early spring bulbs. Alternatively, use as a specimen, pruning the lower branches so the plant develops into a small, multi-stemmed tree. This can be grown as a lawn specimen or sited in the border, surrounded by summer-flowering perennials.

....

Syringa vulgaris 'Belle de Nancy'
Height 8 ft
Spread 6½ ft
Flower size Medium
Scent Strong and pleasant
Color Shell pink
Foliage Matt green
In the garden A good choice for smaller spaces and urban gardens
As a cut flower A beautiful subject, particularly in a pastel arrangement

Banquise

While some flowers and colors can become dated, Banquise is not one of them. Now in its thirteenth decade, it has no intention of showing its age. As elegant and freshly minted as it was when it left the Lemoine Nursery in 1905, it could still stroll along any contemporary catwalk, with cool aplomb and lashings of *je ne sais quoi*.

In the same vein as other geographically-inspired lilac names, such as Etna and Mont Blanc, the French word *banquise* means "ice floe," so florists can riff off this evocative concept, cut it by the armful and combine it with fresh blues and a little green or violet to recreate a polar scene.

Syringa vulgaris 'Banquise'
Height Up to 10 ft
Spread Up to 8 ft
Flower size Large
Scent A floral sensation
Color Creamy white
Foliage Neatly pointed leaves in an unobtrusive shade of green
In the garden Pretty and fresh
As a cut flower Striking and adaptable

Mrs Edward Harding

If you only have room for one lilac in your garden, Mrs Edward Harding is a fine choice indeed. Compact rather than sprawling, it will grow into a nice, bushy little tree, adorned with a delightfully bold reddish-purple froth in late spring and providing useful structure during the rest of the year.

While it will make a lovely foil to summer perennials when sited at the back of an herbaceous border, it is also at home in the shrubbery or as part of a collection where it can be underplanted with snowdrops, epimediums and cyclamen for a bold splash of winter and early spring color before the fragrant double lilac flowers emerge.

Mrs Edward Harding holds two RHS Awards of Garden Merit.

....

Syringa vulgaris 'Mrs Edward Harding'
Height 10–13 ft
Spread 10–13 ft
Flower size Large
Scent Intensely sweet and delicious
Color Purple
Foliage Elegantly rounded with pointed tips
In the garden Grow as a small, multi-stemmed tree or back-of-border plant
As a cut flower The dense, textured panicles provide a real hit of color

Firmament

Introduced in 1932 by Émile Lemoine of the famous French lilac-breeding family, Firmament is a thing of beauty.

The flowers are cerulean blue, the shade of summer skies and fluffy clouds, and while the plummy buds suggest just a whisper of thunder on the horizon, the overall impression is one of lightness, brightness and optimism.

The older lilac varieties tend to be larger than more modern cultivars, but the bonus of size is that the flowers can be cut by the armful without diminishing the garden display and once the early summer blooming is finished the plant should be strong enough to hold its own among a parcel of later glories, such as *Clematis* 'Niobe' or 'Polish Spirit', or moderately sized climbing roses.

Firmament received an Award of Garden Merit from the Royal Horticultural Society in 1993.

Syringa vulgaris 'Firmament'
Height 10 ft
Spread 13 ft
Flower size Medium
Scent Very attractive
Color Sky blue
Foliage Mid-green
In the garden Use as a specimen or as part of a wonderfully frothy mixed spring display
As a cut flower Like a little patch of heaven brought indoors

Mme F. Morel

In the path to success, notoriety or renown, one skill or achievement can eclipse all others to become what one is remembered for.

For a polymath this might be a source of frustration, but it is fair to say that plantsmen tend not to have a single obsession. It may be snowdrops or roses that brings them to prominence, but their equally stellar work with pulmonarias or penstemons, for example, can be eclipsed.

Thus, although Françisque Morel is best known for breeding clematis, he must have been delightfully diverted by lilacs, too, judging by his handiwork in this quarter.

Sumptuous Mme F. Morel, which must surely have been named for his wife, is a lilac that has stood the test of time. Age does not wither the perfection of her petals, which are the most delicious, clear lavender-mauve in color and exquisitely fine in substance. History does not record much about the lady herself, but immortality certainly becomes her.

....

Syringa vulgaris 'Mme F. Morel'
Height Up to 10 ft
Spread Up to 8 ft
Flower size Large
Scent Exquisite
Color Shell pink
Foliage Dull apple green
In the garden An old variety that has stood the test of time
As a cut flower An extremely showy bloom that looks fantastic in a vase

Agincourt Beauty

While most lilacs are dramatic in full flower, Agincourt Beauty is a particularly outstanding creature. The color is delightful and the shrub hardy and easy to grow, but what is really striking is the lush and lavish quality of the bloom.

Tight, damson-colored buds open into flowers that are a delicious, gray-brushed violet and both vast and magnificent. The panicles are dense, weighed heavy with florets that can be up to 1½ inches across – some of the largest of any lilac known. This cultivar is both a bold subject in the garden, beloved by butterflies, and ideal to arrange in a heavy-bottomed vase as part of a single-variety arrangement, or perhaps with smaller white lilacs as a contrast.

Agincourt Beauty prefers cooler summer conditions, with plenty of sun and good drainage around the roots. It does not do particularly well in hot and humid conditions.

Despite the French connotations of the name (the Battle of Agincourt, in 1415, was a decisive victory of the English over the French in the Hundred Years War), the notably more peaceful Agincourt Beauty was bred in Ontario, USA, by Leonard Slater and was introduced in 1968.

....

Syringa vulgaris 'Agincourt Beauty'
Height 8–10 ft
Spread 6–8 ft
Flower size Large
Scent Wonderfully fragrant
Color Smoky lavender
Foliage Fresh green
In the garden Bold in full bloom
As a cut flower Fabulously dramatic

Sensation

Bursting onto the garden stage in early summer, this bold and striking lilac cultivar lives up to its name.

One of the most distinctive varieties available, the claret-infused buds open into single, simple flowers; each light damson petal edged with a margin of clear white.

Left to itself, it is a shrubby, deciduous plant that will form a substantial bush, but it can be trained to form a small tree or "legged up" by removing some of the lower branches. This can create space for underplanting and extending the season of interest, perhaps with spring bulbs, hellebores and evergreen ferns.

Attractive to wildlife and ideal for cutting, it is also sometimes known as Purple Sensation.

Syringa vulgaris 'Sensation'
Height Up to 13 ft
Spread Up to 13 ft
Flower size Medium to large
Scent Very fragrant
Color Red-purple with a white margin
Foliage Narrowish, heart-shaped leaves
In the garden Good in a shrub border or as an informal hedge
As a cut flower Elegant mixed with pink peonies and teamed with soft foliage

Primrose

A refreshing change to the usual *Syringa* palette of mauve, pink and white, Primrose produces rounded panicles of subtly mutable flowers. These start off as tight buds, the color of clotted cream, opening into flowers that are buttercream-white in youth; these develop as they mature, becoming richer and deeper, eventually surpassing even the pale shade of wild primroses and evoking all the sunshine and flowers of spring, although the petal margins remain pale.

An established and widely grown variety, floriferous Primrose grows large with time, so give it the space it needs, ideally at the back of the border. The flowers can be cut for pretty posies and while they look delightful alone, it can pay to experiment with other seasonal blooms such as late tulips or early roses, or contrast the creamy flowers with other, plummier lilacs.

Primrose received an Award of Garden Merit from the RHS in 1950.

Syringa vulgaris 'Primrose'
Height 10–13 ft
Spread 10–13 ft
Flower size Large
Scent Sublime
Color Buttery primrose yellow
Foliage A lovely green foil for the delicate flowers
In the garden Great cottage garden plant, particularly at the back of the border
As a cut flower Charming as part of a fresh, late spring arrangement

Znamya Lenina
syn. Banner of Lenin

Although many lilacs embrace pink in its various forms, shades of red are more unusual. Yet when Leonid Kolesnikov bred handsome Znamya Lenina in Russia, at some point prior to 1936, there must have been something about it to justify the evocative name, which translates to English as Banner of Lenin. Or perhaps it just felt like a lilac-breeding revolution when he first saw it flower.

The color is strong, a red-purple that might, in the right light, hint at the red flag of the Soviet Union, or at least make some sort of patriotic statement in a country where lilac research is actively encouraged and supported.

A heavy bloomer and densely clothed with single florets, this is a plant of style and substance, and one of the best to come out of Russia to date.

Syringa vulgaris 'Znamya Lenina' syn. 'Banner of Lenin'
Height 10 ft
Spread 10 ft
Flower size Large
Scent Sweet and heady
Color An eye-popping red-magenta
Foliage Lush, heart-shaped leaves
In the garden A really good grower
As a cut flower Beautiful on its own, or soften the intensity by adding other flowers and foliage

Edith Cavell

As a Frenchman living and working in occupied France in the First World War, it is fair to say that Émile Lemoine was not a huge fan of the German invaders. In naming the lilac Edith Cavell, as with Général Pershing, he made one of a number of statements that could be viewed as either quietly political or commemorative, honoring notable figures of the times.

Edith Cavell was a British nurse who worked in Belgium. During the war she became a prominent figure in her field, training other nurses in the latest medical advancements and apparently declaring, "I can't stop where there are lives to be saved."

But her compassion, strong ethics and devout mindset were her undoing. She began sheltering British and French soldiers, in total helping around 200 individuals escape to England. In 1915, she was arrested for treason and, despite being a foreigner and amid vocal international calls for mercy, she was charged and executed by the Germans.

The case was well-publicized and became used in propaganda and as a tool for recruitment against the Germans. After all, what red-blooded man would not enlist to fight a country that would shoot innocent women? But Edith Cavell was courageous and dignified to the last, saying, "Patriotism is not enough. I must have no hatred or bitterness towards anyone."

Released in 1916, this lilac is lauded as one of the finest white doubles available. It makes a hardy and upright shrub or small tree, which bears huge clusters of exquisite double flowers, but it can be prone to leaf roll necrosis, so plant it away from busy roads.

....

Syringa vulgaris 'Edith Cavell'
Height 11½ ft
Spread 8 ft
Flower size Medium to large
Scent Divine
Color White
Foliage Large heart-shaped leaves
In the garden Has stood the test of time
As a cut flower A real performer and ideal in a bridal bouquet

Monge

Fabulous, fragrant and a wonderful shade of deep purple, Monge is a fine lilac indeed.

In the garden it forms a moderately sized, upright bush, which produces large and sumptuous flower heads in late April or May. But it really comes into its own as a cut flower.

A few stems in a modest vase are simple and elegant, but the flowers are that sort of desirable hue that will go with anything, so use them to anchor more vibrant colors, such as pink and orange, or combine with other lilacs in purples, blues and violets for a visual feast as well as an olfactory one.

Monge was introduced by the Lemoine family in France, in 1913.

Syringa vulgaris 'Monge'
Height 10–12 ft
Spread 8–10 ft
Flower size Large
Scent Ravishing
Color A rich, bold purple
Foliage Blue-green and slightly glossy; mildew-resistant
In the garden Makes an impressive splash of color
As a cut flower Excellent; both bold and dramatic

Mme Lemoine

When you think about the legendary, lilac-breeding Lemoine family, it is the chaps who get most of the attention. Victor, Émile and Henri have rightly gone down in the annals of horticultural history for their astonishingly profuse breeding work, not just with lilacs, but with hydrangeas, too.

Yet Marie Lemoine was not a silent partner in proceedings. And, when Victor decided that he would use the *Syringa vulgaris* 'Azurea Plena' that was growing in their garden as the seed parent (and we are assuming that it was his idea here, not hers or, quite possibly, a joint effort) it was Marie who did the legwork.

The Azurea Plena was large and the double flowers blessed with awkwardly twisted petals; these had to be painstakingly parted to anoint the stigmas with pollen from the finest single lilac cultivars the experimenting pair could get their hands on. And it was Marie, younger and nimbler than her husband, who scaled the ladder to perform the cross.

So it is only fair that a particularly fine lilac, introduced in 1890, bears her name. A neat and free-flowering double, it looks beautiful in the garden and possibly even better in the vase.

Mme Lemoine received an RHS Award of Garden Merit in 1937, 1891 and 1897.

....

Syringa vulgaris 'Mme Lemoine'
Height Up to 10 ft
Spread Up to 8 ft
Flower size Large
Scent Fills the air with perfume
Color White with a touch of cream
Foliage Green
In the garden No trouble at all
As a cut flower Versatile and lovely

GROWING AND CARE

WHILE LILACS ARE UNDOUBTEDLY CHARMING AND NOSTALGIC, THEY ARE ALSO DISGRACEFULLY EASY TO GROW. CERTAINLY, THEY HAVE PREFERENCES AND THEY MAY WELL BENEFIT FROM A TACTICAL TRIM NOW AND AGAIN, BUT CHOOSE THE RIGHT PLANT AND PUT IT IN THE RIGHT PLACE — WITH PLENTY OF SUN AND DRAINAGE — AND THIS EASY-GOING SHRUB WILL GROW, THRIVE AND BLOOM FOR MANY YEARS TO COME.

Cultivation

With a very few exceptions, *Syringa* are happy-go-lucky characters that, a few minor needs fulfilled, will give great pleasure. But needs they have, and preferences too, and getting to know your shrub and your climate is key to getting the very best results. First of all, lilacs like sun, so aim for at least six hours a day, preferably more in colder places. In hotter areas, meanwhile, or on very sharply drained soil, a little bit of shade can be of benefit. This will help the flowers last longer and prevent the colors fading too soon.

Lilacs will flower better after a moderately chilly winter than after a warm one so in temperate climates, such as the UK and much of Northern Europe, they are well-adapted. But gardeners in areas with greater extremes of temperature need not despair.

The ×*hyacinthiflora* lilacs bred by Canadian Frank Skinner are particularly resistant to cold, and it seems fair to assume that anything that originates in Russia will have a robust attitude to winter. Warmth is a greater problem, and in the southern US states or parts of the Southern Hemisphere, insufficient chilling may be an issue. But certain varieties, such as the warm-winter ×*hyacinthiflora* lilacs, where *S. vulgaris* is crossed with *S. oblata* subsp. *oblata* (page 211), are more tolerant of this than others.

Secondly, lilacs love good drainage. Those who garden on light soil, sandy loam, on shale or even a bit of a slope will receive this news with joy, and proceed in the confidence that their plants will thrive. But if you have damp ground or heavy clay that puddles in winter and cracks in summer, all is not lost.

With the exception of *Syringa emodi*, the Himalayan lilac, which rather likes moisture, the genus *Syringa* will not thrive in waterlogged ground or bog. However, this can be circumvented by building up a mound of soil and planting the shrub on top of it, so drainage will be improved. Alternatively, lilacs can be planted in raised beds or in large containers.

Selecting varieties

Lilacs are consistent in that they all bloom in spring and they like sun and hate waterlogging, as discussed on the previous page. So having chosen a color you like, the key considerations when selecting a variety for the garden are its ultimate size, any tendency for suckering that might make the plant more suitable for a larger garden, and its tolerance both to cold and to heat.

While some varieties are reasonably compact and make good hedges or even container plants, others are relatively mighty and eventually form a substantial shrub or even a small tree. They are also long-lived, so getting the choice of lilac right first time and planting it in the right place saves trouble down the line.

One of the more charming qualities of lilacs is their tolerance to cold, a liking for light notwithstanding. Most are comfortable in USDA Zones 4–7; but they are not just tolerant of cold. To flower properly they actively need around 42 cool days, or 1,000 hours, of temperatures below 50 degrees Fahrenheit (10 degrees Celsius). As a result, in very cold areas such as parts of Canada or Russia, they are one of the few flowering shrubs that offer gardeners a wide range of choice. Fewer varieties are available for gardeners in persistently warm areas, but they do exist.

If you are gardening at the margins of *Syringa* tolerance, there are a number of tricks that will increase the chances of success. In hot regions,

---

HARDINESS

There are a range of charts and tables that indicate what level of chill a plant will tolerate. Two useful systems are produced by the United States Department of Agriculture (USDA) and the RHS, which range from tropical to extremely hardy.

USDA
Zone 3 -40°C to -34°C (-40°F to -30°F)
Zone 4 -34°C to -29°C (-30°F to -20°F)
Zone 5 -29°C to -23°C (-20°F to -10°F)
Zone 6 -23°C to -18°C (-10°F to 0°F)
Zone 7 -18°C to -12°C (0°F to 10°F)
Zone 8 -12°C to -7°C (10°F to 20°F)
Zone 9 -7°C to -1°C (20°F to 30°F)

RHS
H3 to -5°C (23°F), half hardy
H4 to -10°C (14°F), hardy in an average winter
H5 to -15°C (5°F), hardy in a cold winter
H6 to -20°C (-4°F), hardy in a very cold winter
H7 colder than -20°C (-4°F), very hardy

Many lilacs are fully hardy, tolerating chill to approximately USDA 4–7. Where varieties may be less hardy, this is indicated in the plant profiles on pages 34–205.

withholding water from the plant will force it into dormancy; then, when watered at a later date, it will bloom without a period of cold.

In cold areas, insufficient hardiness is not generally too much of a problem, but the more early-flowering types risk buds and flowers being scorched by late frosts. If this is a hazard, avoid planting in frost pockets and, where possible, site your lilacs on higher ground where they won't be subject to flows of cold air. If temperatures are forecast to dip after the flowers arrive, spreading a blanket or other insulating layer over the top of the plant can help, as long as it is not too big. Local experts will usually be happy to advise.

Below I outline some of the main species and hybrids of lilac, their requirements and their characteristics. You will find more details on size, color and tolerance of a number of key cultivars in the profile chapters.

Syringa vulgaris

Native to south-eastern Europe, *Syringa vulgaris* is known as the common lilac for good reason. The first to be bred and hybridized, it is widespread throughout the world. Hybrids of *S. vulgaris* are often generically known as French lilacs in honor of the extensive breeding work done by the Lemoine family, between the 1800s and 1955 (pages 18–19).

In its wild and untamed state, *S. vulgaris* is a tall, spreading, suckering shrub that grows to around 12 feet tall by 8 feet wide. Its main period of interest is when it is blooming, after which it fades into the background. Its core temperature range is USDA Zones 4–7, but some cultivars will flower in the extremes of USDA Zones 3 and 8.

Syringa × chinensis

Despite its name, this cultivar is a hybrid of *Syringa vulgaris* and *S. protolaciniata* and was discovered in the 1770s in the botanic garden in Rouen, France. As a result, it is often referred to as the Chinese lilac or Rouen lilac.

Tough and adaptable, with small, green leaves, it forms a round shrub about 12 feet tall and equally wide, and bears delicate, heavily scented flowers. Compared to *S. vulgaris*, it suckers less and the flowers appear later, making it less susceptible to frost. It flowers in USDA Zones 3–9.

Syringa × hyacinthiflora

Known as the American lilac, Canadian lilac, or sometimes as the early hybrid, the ×*hyacinthiflora* lilacs were created by Victor Lemoine, by crossing a double form of common lilac, *Syringa vulgaris* 'Azurea Plena' with *S. oblata* subsp. *oblata* in 1876.

This group of lilacs will bloom in USDA Zone 7–9, warm winter areas, and the flowers arrive earlier than *S. vulgaris*, which usefully extends the lilac season, although it does make them vulnerable to frost damage. In autumn, the foliage turns orange and dark red-purple.

A more compact and cold-hardy form was created when Frank Skinner crossed *S. vulgaris* with *S. oblata* subsp. *dilatata*, which will cope in USDA Zone 2 – these are often known in the USA as Canadian lilacs and in Canada as American lilacs.

Syringa emodi

A large plant, growing to around 15 feet tall, the Himalayan lilac, was discovered in the early 1830s towards the western end of the mountain range, near the Kurram Valley on the border of Afghanistan and Pakistan. Unlike most lilacs, it positively enjoys rich, moist soil, and will sulk and may drop its leaves if conditions get too dry underfoot. It also prefers some shade.

The flowers are gorgeous; white, delicate and airy, but they bring themselves down to earth with a less-than-delicious scent.

Syringa josikaea

The Hungarian lilac is one of just two species that are native to Europe, but compared to *Syringa vulgaris*, it is much less well-known. Although usefully late-blooming, it is less tolerant of drought and poor soil conditions, the flowers are smaller and less fragrant and it is slightly less hardy than its common cousin.

Syringa josikaea is now considered endangered in its native habitat of the Carpathian Mountains.

Syringa pubescens subsp. *pubescens*, formerly known as *S. meyeri*

This naturally dwarf lilac was "discovered" in 1908 by American Frank Meyer, in a garden near Beijing. Reliable in its flowering – even sometimes producing a scattered second flush of blooms – it develops maroon autumn color and is hardy in USDA Zones 3–7. Generally, this is a healthy and tolerant shrub which has grown in popularity because of its small size.

Syringa × prestoniae

Winter-hardy in the extreme, tolerating conditions down to USDA Zone 2, the Preston lilacs are named for hybridizer Isabella Preston, who crossed *Syringa villosa* with *S. komarowii* subsp. *reflexa*, to create a series of tall shrubs or small trees that flower a week or so after the common lilac.

Syringa pubescens

This species of lilac is native to China and is named for its leaves, which are hairy, or pubescent, on the underside. It is naturally dwarf, just 3–6 feet tall, and slow-growing, so it is a good choice for a container or low hedge. A hardy, healthy, non-suckering shrub, the scented flowers are produced later than most lilacs, arriving in early summer, so they are rarely lost to frost.

Syringa villosa

Syringa villosa produces a large shrub around 12 feet tall which is hardy to USDA Zone 2, highly floriferous and tolerant of drought and salt, so the average-to-objectionable scent of the flowers can probably be forgiven. It was discovered in China by French missionary Pierre d'Incarville in 1750.

Buying lilacs

Lilacs are frequently offered for sale in full bloom as part of a tempting display of spring highlights and, as a result, they are most usually bought potted up and in growth. But if you are looking for something out of the ordinary, specialists and collectors may have plants available at any time of year, and suppliers of hedges and landscaping plants may also sell lilacs when dormant, as bare-root shrubs in winter.

Regardless of how you buy your plant, make sure that it is healthy. If it is in leaf, the leaves should be a good green color and the stems should be firm, smooth and with no evidence of rot, dieback or mechanical damage. Check carefully for pests and diseases – lilacs are hearty plants but it pays to make sure.

Avoid specimens with dead stems and lots of moss growth around the top of the pot; this could indicate damp conditions or that the plant has been left standing in water, which lilacs hate. And don't be shy about checking the roots – carefully upend the pot, supporting the plant with your hand; the roots should be well-grown and fibrous, with white growing tips when the plant is in leaf.

Plants bought by mail order may well arrive bare-rooted, in which case unpack them immediately and immerse the roots in a bucket of water, in a shady spot, for an hour or so. If you are unable to plant them at once, heel the plants into the ground by digging a shallow trench, lying the roots in it and then backfilling with soil. Alternatively, pot them up until such a time as you can deal with them properly.

Grafted lilacs

Grafting is the process whereby the top of one plant is spliced onto the roots of another. It is a commonly used technique to control size in tree fruit and, in the past, lilacs might have been found grafted onto the roots of *Fraxinus* species, privet or other lilacs. Considerable testing has settled on the Hungarian lilac, *Syringa josikaea*, as the most suitable rootstock, because it has proven itself less susceptible to disease than privet and less liable to sucker than other lilac species.

With older plants and those not sold as standards, you can tell if a lilac is grafted as there will be a rounded knobble or swelling just above the roots, and the bark may look different above and below it. From a modern point of view, grafts are often considered more trouble than they are worth, acting as an entry point for disease, risking incompatibility, and often with the tendency for the rootstock to develop suckers that will then grow more strongly and overwhelm the named cultivar. As a result, most plants are now sold on their own roots. But if you do find yourself with a grafted plant, the convention now is to plant the bush with the graft below the surface of the soil, which will encourage the scion to develop its own roots.

Grafts are now primarily used where the plant is sold as a standard – a formal way of growing the plant as a mop-headed bush on top of a long, straight stem – or in expert hands as a temporary solution to conserving propagation material.

Planting and moving lilacs

Like most shrubs, lilacs will do best when planted into good soil, where they can settle in and grow away immediately. In practice, this means picking a moment when the soil is reasonably warm, not too wet, not too dry and not frozen solid.

Theoretically you can plant out your potted lilac whenever you receive it, but it is generally best to leave disturbing the roots until spring or autumn. Very cold, wet or dry conditions will stress the plant and it may not thrive. If you do plant out your lilac in summer, water it frequently and thoroughly afterwards.

Choose a congenial location with plenty of sun and with enough room for the plant to grow. Lilacs are tough but they like good, well-drained soil if they can get it. Poor soils can be improved with a little well-rotted manure or garden compost, and heavy ones lightened by digging through a bucket or two of grit and some organic matter. Perversely, very rich soils can actually inhibit flowering, so don't overdo the nutrition.

Water the plant well by immersing the roots in a bucket, then dig a hole approximately twice the size of the root ball; tease or spread out the roots, and settle into the hole so that the top of the soil that was in the pot – or the mark on the stem where the plant was dug – is at ground level. Backfill with earth and firm around the plant, then water it in and, ideally, add a layer of organic mulch to retain moisture.

While it is conventional to move most plants when they are dormant or growing slowly, even quite large lilacs have been successfully moved in late summer and some practitioners will advise that lilacs can be moved at any time of year, except when the plant is in bloom.

The trick seems to be to ensure that the shrub retains plenty of root and that its new home has good drainage and the soil is relatively light; the plant should then be watered well and frequently to encourage the growth of shallow, fibrous feeding roots. It can be a good idea to cut back top growth somewhat, to compensate for any severed roots, then mulch well with chipped bark, straw or something similarly friable.

Feeding and mulching

Lilacs are a tolerant bunch, and while good soil is a bonus, they will put up with really quite poor conditions. As a result, lavishing them with love and nitrogen in the hope of getting even bigger and better displays may very often have the reverse effect.

A surplus of nitrogen – the "N" element in NPK fertilizer – will create lots of lush, sappy growth. This makes the plant more vulnerable to pests and bad weather. Overfed and overexcited, it may then flower poorly and can develop a tendency to sucker.

So if your plant is growing amazingly well but flowers are few, think about its diet. Even if it is not being directly fed, other things can pump up the nitrogen level, including rich top dressing with manure in borders, feeding surrounding grass, or even a urinating pet.

The moral of the story is, therefore, to improve the ground moderately when planting and, if you feel you must feed, do so just after flowering, using a high-potash feed such as tomato food (in an NPK fertilizer, this is where the "P" is assigned a high number).

A layer of organic mulch will reduce competition from grass and weeds, and delineate the shrub's personal space, as well as keeping the ground in good condition and draining well. If you want to create a formal look, arrange a ring of cardboard or newspaper around the lilac to the edge of the canopy and cover with 2–4 inches of bark mulch.

GROWING IN CONTAINERS

Lilacs are often hefty shrubs, and even the daintier ones have spreading roots, so they are not necessarily the perfect container specimen. But if you must have a potted lilac, there are a few rules for success.

First, choose one of the smaller cultivars, such as *Syringa meyeri* 'Palibin' or newly developed Flowerfesta® Pink or *Syringa* Tinkerbelle®. Then choose a large container; this will need to be an absolute minimum of 20 inches wide and 16 inches deep, but larger is better, not just to accommodate the plant, but to help it withstand heat and cold and retain moisture and nutrients better.

Use a soil-based, peat-free growing medium designed for mature plants, this should be both water-retentive and free-draining. It is quite straightforward to make your own, mixing together good garden soil with a proportion of compost and some grit – adding more for heavy soil, and less for light soil. Plant your lilac into the container, leaving a 1-inch gap at the top, firm the soil and water well. Although it will need at least four to six hours of direct sunlight per day, a sheltered and partly shady location will reduce the need for watering.

In temperate climates potted lilacs should overwinter outdoors without difficulty, but in places that suffer from long periods of intense cold, protection may be needed to stop the roots freezing. Create an insulating layer by wrapping the pot in straw or newspaper, or burying the root ball or the whole container in the ground. In really arctic conditions, the container can be brought into a shed or greenhouse, but it is better not to, if possible, as lilacs need a period of cold to initiate flowering (page 210).

Propagating lilacs

Some commercial nurseries produce plants by the thousands, and tissue culture techniques can be used to make a particular cultivar rapidly and widely available, but there are two straightforward ways that a gardener or collector can make new lilacs at home – one is by sowing seeds, the other is by cloning the parent.

When seeds are produced, the genetic material of the parents is recombined to create new individuals with some of the characteristics of both. If you have time on your hands, it can be fun to create deliberate crosses of named varieties; superior parents will result in better quality offspring.

Sow ripe seeds into containers filled with good seed compost and equipped with drainage holes, then cover with a bit more compost and water well. Dormancy is broken by a process of chilling and thawing, so leave the container outside somewhere sheltered until shoots appear.

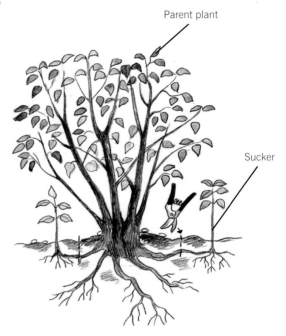

Parent plant

Sucker

**CUT THE ROOTED SUCKER
TO CREATE A NEW PLANT**

A faster way to produce new individuals of named varieties or multiplying a favorite cultivar is to take a division or cutting and grow it on to produce a new plant.

Division: This is easiest in varieties that form lots of suckers at the roots. Wait until the sucker is established, or is at least two years old, then dig it up carefully, going deep to obtain as much root as possible and severing it from the parent with a knife, sharp spade or secateurs, if necessary.

Layering: Choose a low-growing branch and bend it flat, pinning it down with a hoop of wire so that the branch remains in contact with the soil. With time, new roots will develop, but the process can be accelerated by creating a wound in the underside of the branch and dusting it with

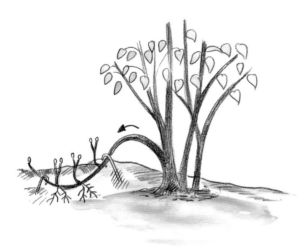

**STIMULATE ROOT PRODUCTION
BY LAYERING LOW-GROWING BRANCHES**

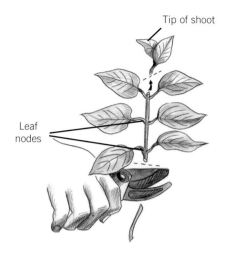

Tip of shoot

Leaf nodes

CUT STEM BELOW A LEAF NODE

hormone rooting powder. Burying the section of the stem to be rooted can also help. When roots have developed, which may take a couple of years, cut the original branch and transplant the new plant to the desired location.

Softwood cuttings: Lilacs vary by variety in how easily they will root from cuttings, but it is always worth a try. After flowering, take a new, flexible shoot, the thickness of a pencil and about 4–6 inches long, and trim the bottom to just below a leaf node. Then remove the tip and surplus leaves and insert it into a pot of gritty compost – you can put several cuttings in the same pot. Using rooting hormone can improve success and, ideally, take a number of cuttings to guard against failure.

Place in a clear plastic bag to create a humid environment, then leave in a bright location out of direct sunlight. Roots should appear in a month or two, at which point the lilac can be potted on or planted out to overwinter.

REMOVE LEAVES

PLUNGE INTO A POT OF COMPOST

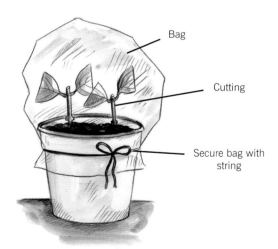

Bag

Cutting

Secure bag with string

PUT IN A PLASTIC BAG

Pruning

Most shrubs and trees benefit from occasional pruning; it helps keep them compact and in good shape and can help stop them outgrowing their space. It also helps stimulate growth, generating a new supply of flowering wood, and helping to ensure consistent blooming.

Like other early-flowering shrubs, such as *Forsythia*, flowering currant or *Ribes sanguineum, and Philadelphus* or mock orange, lilacs should be pruned in late spring or early summer just after they have finished flowering.

The reason for this is that they form their flower and leaf buds in summer, so pruning at any other time of year risks cutting off all the flowers for next spring.

REMOVE STEMS AND BRANCHES
AS NECESSARY

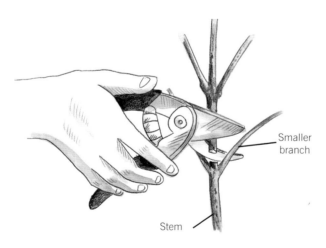

Smaller branch

Stem

PRUNING WHERE TWO
BRANCHES JOIN

PRUNING ABOVE A BUD

Wild or naturalized lilacs will continue flowering in their own sweet way and, up to a point, get larger and larger. At home, the plant can be pruned at a frequency to suit the gardener and the space available. In small gardens, it can be a good idea to prune annually. Every few years is fine, too – it will just be a bigger plant, and therefore a bigger job, when you get around to it.

Use a sharp, clean pruning saw and secateurs to remove any dead and diseased wood, then, on mature plants, reduce the number of congested stems as necessary. When pruning to improve shape, remove inward-facing branches and reduce the length of wayward stems by cutting just above a bud or where two branches join. You can also remove thicker, older, more upright stems at ground level if they are too numerous or you wish to create a floriferous bush rather than something more tree-like.

The other thing to consider is removing suckers that emerge from below the graft on grafted lilacs. If you let them grow the resulting stems will eventually flower, but the flowers will be those of the rootstock rather than the cultivated variety, and may, eventually, come to dominate. If you have a large and neglected lilac that needs renovating, do so gradually by cutting out a number of the oldest stems each year. Decide whether you want to achieve a bush or a tree, then, depending on the scale of the plant in question, a certain amount of individual license can be deployed. If you are happy to sacrifice some of the following year's flowers, renovation pruning can be done at any time.

When pruning any plant, it's a good idea to stand back regularly and assess your handiwork. Avoid cutting out all the low branches, as these will carry their flowers at eye and nose level and, finally, know when to stop – you can always come back next year.

Pests, diseases and other problems

One of the most trouble-free and laid-back plants available, lilacs thrive with very little attention, so they are ideal for low-maintenance schemes and organic gardeners alike.

Of course, there are always a few creatures keen to take a tactical nibble, but growing a plant that is healthy and resilient is the best way to battle this, along with a vigilant attitude.

Different areas of a country or continent can present different horticultural challenges and problems, and pests that are prevalent in one area may be absent or insignificant in another. The information below, therefore, is designed to provide guidance and it is a good idea to seek out local expert gardeners and visit lilac collections for advice on your specific issues.

Pests

One person's idea of a pest is another person's idea of wildlife, and while some beetles, bugs and other beasts can undoubtedly cause damage if their populations are allowed to build up, the fact that they do so is indicative of their place in nature, often at the bottom of the food chain, where they support a host of larger creatures that are more dear to our hearts.

Growing the plant well, so that it is strong, healthy and able to bounce back from any attack, is key. It is also a good idea to keep an eye out for early signs of trouble – and familiarize yourself with your enemy at a local level. Insects that are

an issue in Europe, lilac leaf miner, for example, may be a minor irritation in the USA, while cicadas are not a garden pest in Britain. Many other insects may happily include lilac as part of a diverse diet, but do not usually present a major challenge to cultivation.

LILAC LEAF MINING MOTH

Caloptilia syringella is a small insect – around 0.4–0.5 inches across – with brown and white wings. The caterpillars feed within the leaves of plants including lilac and privet (*Ligustrum*), and it is more prevalent in the UK and Europe than in the Americas.

The "mine" starts off as a blotch on the leaf, usually in midsummer. This is occupied by several green caterpillars that burrow and forage around inside it, before breaking out and causing the leaf to roll up from the tip. They then secure this tube with silk, creating a safe haven within which to finish their development.

The first generation pupates when the fully grown caterpillars are about 0.3 inches long, and a second generation appears in late summer or early autumn. These overwinter as pupae.

Leaf miners are unlikely to cause serious damage or disfigurement to lilac trees and there are plenty of predators, such as small birds, which will happily forage on the caterpillars. On a domestic level, the best thing to do – if you want to do anything – is pick off affected leaves and dispose of them in the rubbish bin or by burning.

LILAC BORER

Although its stripy abdomen resembles that of a wasp, the lilac borer, *Podosesia syringae* is, in fact, a clearwing moth that is endemic throughout the continental USA. The larvae feed upon the same woody species as do those of the lilac leaf miner, growing up to 1 inch long and burrowing into the sapwood and phloem to create galleries in the trunks and larger branches.

Given that insecticide sprays are indiscriminate in what they kill, the best thing to do is to keep the plant healthy and resilient and guard against wounds inflicted by strimmers and mowers, which create an easy access point. Using pheromone traps in spring will reduce the population of adult males, which will then not be able to mate and create a new generation.

THRIPS

An occasional problem in warm climates, thrips are small, long-bodied, sap-sucking black insects. When there is an infestation, leaves can become dull and silvery, and spots of black excrement may be visible – you can check for their presence by shaking a branch over a piece of white paper and inspecting the results.

Because they are so small, thrips dislike moist locations so they can be kept in check by spraying or misting the plant with water, and by frequent showers of rain. Cold winters will also slow them down.

Diseases

While diseases exist, they are not generally considered to be a huge problem with lilacs, as long as the plants are well-grown and cared for. Given plenty of fresh air and an environment that is neither too damp nor too dry, it is an unfortunate lilac that will succumb – although they can suffer from the growth of twiggy masses known as "witches' broom" and they can be susceptible to pollution. Non-host-specific diseases, such as sudden oak death and verticillium wilt, can affect lilacs, but they don't single them out in particular.

POWDERY MILDEW

Powdery mildew is unsightly rather than disastrous and it tends to appear on plants later in the season on mature foliage. Powdery mildew is, in fact, several types of fungus, it is often more of a problem in warm areas and in dry summers when plants may be more drought-stressed and less resilient.

Powdery mildew is common in gardens and since it does not kill the plant there is no real point in trying to get rid of it, although if the weather has been dry, it can help to give your lilac a good drink when you first spot it. You can prevent a reoccurrence by pruning the bush so that it has an open frame and good air circulation.

LILAC BLIGHT

Bacterial blight of lilacs, *Pseudomonas syringae* var. *syringae*, is more common in cool, wet areas and on heavy soils. It first appears as blotches on the leaves, going on to cause distorted and blackened foliage, and flowers that turn brown and limp. It is more common in warmer areas of the USA than it is in the UK.

It does not generally appear every year, so prune out any affected branches and improve the air circulation around the plant, making sure to clean your tools before and afterwards.

Fungal blights also exist and include *Phytophthora syringae* and *Ascochyta syringae*.

HONEY FUNGUS

There are several species of *Armillaria*, and these attack the roots of a range of trees and shrubs, including viburnums, weigelas, pines, oaks and rhododendrons. Weak or aging specimens are more vulnerable.

If your plant looks unwell, dies suddenly or the leaves become smaller and paler over time,

look for a white fungal growth between the bark and the wood near the base – carefully peel back a section if you are unsure. You may also discover black, stringy "bootlace" rhizomorphs protruding from the roots. In late summer or autumn, yellow-brown mushrooms may appear around the base or stump of the plant.

There is no cure, so remove severely affected plants and don't replant lilacs in the same area.

POLLUTION

Syringa as a genus is not very tolerant of pollution, and emissions from industry and particularly road traffic can cause a condition called leaf roll necrosis, where the leaf margins start to curl and the leaves may fall.

Site lilacs away from busy roads and other sources of pollution where possible.

Mammals and mechanical damage

There are a number of ways in which grazing, gnawing or burrowing animals can cause problems for the gardener. But compared to the ravages of insects or mildews, mammals tend to fly under the radar, which can make their depredations unexpected and upsetting. Even more traumatic, however, is the destructive potential of the unrestrained human operative.

DEER

Browsing and rubbing animals can affect a range of garden plants. Some keen gardeners try to deer-proof their entire gardens, but if this is not feasible, surrounding your young lilac in a tall cage made of chicken wire until it is well established can help. Alternatively, you can experiment with repellents: spraying plants with cayenne pepper in water or Tabasco sauce is sometimes recommended.

RABBITS, MICE AND VOLES

Gnawing creatures can be a real problem for many young shrubs and trees. Rabbits will nibble at new growth and stems both for food and to keep their continuously growing teeth in check. Voles and mice, meanwhile, will set up a winter home around the roots, especially on soft ground where there is plenty of weed cover, and they will dig and nibble merrily away at the base of the tree and the roots, remaining undiscovered until spring when the plant fails to break leaf.

Barriers and application of chilli or other repellents can work, and smaller rodents can be discouraged by firming the plant well into the ground then surrounding the stem with a layer of mulch to suppress the sheltering weeds. It is a good idea to ensure that the mulch is granular or fibrous, rather than using cardboard or similar, as that itself could provide congenial winter shelter for the mice and voles.

MOWERS AND STRIMMERS

It is an unfortunate but almost universal truth that a large number of shrubs and trees are damaged or killed by unskilled or uncaring operators of machinery every year. Mowing the grass is a job often given to the least experienced member of any team, but the pursuit of tidiness can cause nicks, abrasions and total ring-barking of prized lilacs.

So protect your plant any way you can – a tree guard may help, as might staking with large, conspicuous posts, but arguably a combination of rigorously enforced education of the masses and a wide and obvious cleared and mulched area, free of grass, is probably the safest way forward.

GLOSSARY

AGM Award of Garden Merit, given by the Royal Horticultural Society, indicates that the plant is recommended by the society and will perform well in the garden.

Anther The pollen sac at the end of the stamen.

Bicolor Having two colors.

Cultivar A cultivated form of the plant selected for its desirable characteristics.

Deadheading Removing spent flowers from the plant to encourage more blooms.

Dwarf A smaller than usual cultivar of a plant.

Forced, forcing A process by which a plant can be persuaded to flower out of season, usually achieved by modifying periods of cold and light exposure.

Genus A biological classification ranking above species, usually including a cluster of related species.

Hybrid A genetic cross between two different species, genera or cultivars.

Leaf axil The joint between the leaf and the stem.

Pedicel A small stalk, bearing a flower or group of flowers.

pH The measure of acidity or alkalinity.

Phloem A type of vascular tissue in which soluble organic nutrients, including sugars, are moved around a plant.

Plasticity The tendency of individuals of the same genetic makeup to look different from each other when grown under different conditions.

Potash The horticultural term for the element Potassium (K) in water-soluble form. The name comes from the original practice of collecting wood ashes in a container.

Recurved, reflexed Where the petals of a flower are curved backwards, often strongly so.

RHS Abbreviation for the Royal Horticultural Society.

Rootstock A stem with a well-developed root system, to which another plant can be joined to make growth above ground.

Scion A shoot or twig that has been cut for grafting.

Series In botany and plant taxonomy, a series is a rank that lies below genus and above species.

Species A population of individuals that have a high level of genetic similarity and which can interbreed.

Stamen The pollen-producing (male) reproductive organ of a flower. It consists of a filament and an anther.

Stigma The part of a plant's female reproductive system that receives the pollen.

Style The stalk or tube that links the stigma to the ovary.

Suckers Growths that appear from the root system of a plant that will, eventually, develop a shoot and their own roots.

Thyrsus (plural thyrses) In botany, a dense flower cluster, such as a lilac.

Variety A classification of cultivated plants, below subspecies, where there are minor but distinctive and inheritable characteristics exhibited.

Vegetative propagation The process by which plants produce genetically identical new individuals, or clones.

Viable (offspring) The progeny of a hybridization event between two fertile individuals, which are themselves fertile.

INDEX

AUTHOR'S ACKNOWLEDGMENTS

This book is dedicated to Isabella, who lives life in a symphony of blue and mauve.

For me, lilac is one of those flowers that just is. They live – mostly unobtrusively – in the garden; they look lovely in a vase with tulips – particularly the dark purple ones – and pausing for a quick sniff of a wayside flower never fails to fire up the pleasure centers in my brain. It has, therefore, been a great adventure to uncover the mysteries of the ostensibly familiar. But it has not been an easy journey. Like my last book, *Lilies*, *Lilacs* has been created in a pandemic year; restrictions and uncertainly have been the order of the day and it is in such times that heroes make themselves known.

My family has walked beside me on my journey of *Lilacs*, as with *Lilies* and my other books, too. They have been tolerant, supportive and although the creative process is sometimes torrid, they only threatened to stage an intervention once. So huge thanks to Chris and the children to helping me to achieve my goals.

In pursuit of accuracy and detail, my horticultural, botanical and media friends and colleagues, old and new, have been wonderful. Guy Barter at the RHS is always immensely helpful with advice and context. I am also hugely indebted to the luminaries at the International Lilac Society for their generosity with both time and information; Claire Fouquet, Mark DeBard and Robert Zavodny have been unswervingly patient and prompt and have answered all my questions and clarified points of issue with a precision that gladdens the heart. My thanks to you all.

Throughout the challenges of the process, I am grateful for the steadfast support of Clare Double, Sophie Allen, Isabelle Holton, Ellen Simmonds and Lucy Smith at Pavilion. I also much appreciate the editorial hand of Helena Caldon. Thanks to Alice Kennedy-Owen and Sophie Yamamoto for their design skills, and to Somang Lee who creates such beautiful illustrations.

As always, it has been a huge pleasure to work with my friend and colleague Georgianna Lane and her husband, David Phillips. Without their drive and energy and their sheer efficiency, this project must surely have foundered and their ability to produce precisely what is required, as if by magic, is both comforting and astonishing. Even with the strictures of the year, and in the face of poor weather, indifferent blooming and the ever-present threat of the pandemic, they managed to photograph lilacs in both America and in France, emerging triumphant with a magnificent portfolio of varieties. I look forward to our next project together but, more than that, I look forward to seeing them in real life, perhaps in a garden somewhere, and raising a glass to success and the future.

PHOTOGRAPHER'S ACKNOWLEDGMENTS

My sincere thanks, as always, to the publishing, editorial and design teams at Pavilion Books for envisioning this wonderful series and for again choosing me to bring that vision to life in photographs.

Un grand merci to Christophe Nourdin and Katia Astafieff at the Jardin Botanique Jean-Marie Pelt at Nancy, France. Katia welcomed our inquiry and connected us with Christophe, whose expertise was invaluable as to bloom times and when to coordinate our visit. He enabled open access for us to photograph this wonderful collection at the peak time and was unfailing in his enthusiasm and support for the project.

My gratitude to the members and volunteers of Hulda Klager Lilac Society at Hulda Klager Lilac Gardens in Woodland, Washington, for maintaining this important national historic site where a significant selection of the images were photographed.

Thank you to Claire Fouquet for her insightful review of the images, and to Mark L. DeBard for his knowledge and generous use of his images of *Syringa oblata* and Mme F. Morel.

Several key species were photographed at the Jardin des Plantes in Paris.

A flourish, deep bow and tip of the hat to my creative partner, author Naomi Slade. During the course of creating this volume (our second title produced under pandemic restrictions) she persisted even when prospects were bleak, presenting us with dazzling and fittingly lush words to celebrate the glory of lilacs.

Gratitude to my ever-patient family members for their cheerful support of my intense production schedule.

Those familiar with this series will know by now that an invisible third partner, my husband David Phillips, is deeply involved in most every logistic, location and creative decision, and that both Naomi and I realize that this volume likely would not exist without his considerable contributions.

Finally, this is dedicated to Marianna, whose boundless enthusiasm and passion for lilacs inspired this project and who accompanied me during the shooting of a major portion of the book at Hulda Klager Lilac Gardens. I hope you can see it from where you are, Mummy.

26 25 24   5 4 3

Published in the United States of America by
Gibbs Smith
PO Box 667
Layton, Utah 84041
1.800.835.4993 orders
www.gibbs-smith.com

Text copyright © 2022 Naomi Slade
Photography copyright © 2022 Georgianna Lane

ISBN 978-1-4236-6130-6
Library of Congress Control Number: 2021950273

Reproduction by Rival Colour Ltd, UK
Printed and bound in Malaysia by Papercraft Sdn Bhd.

First published in the United Kingdom in 2022 by
Pavilion
43 Great Ormond Street
London
WC1N 3HZ

Throughout this book, every attempt has been
made to refer to each lilac variety by its most
accurate and appropriate name, bearing in mind
breeding, registration and commercial matters,
but with ease of reading in mind. Should any
corrections be necessary, the publisher would
be happy to make them in any future printings.